THE LIFE BOOK OF CHRISTMAS • VOLUME ONE

THE
GLORY
OF
CHRISTMAS

OTHER BOOKS BY THE EDITORS OF LIFE

LIFE World Library

LIFE Nature Library

LIFE Science Library

The LIFE History of the United States

LIFE Pictorial Atlas of the World

The Epic of Man

The Wonders of Life on Earth

The World We Live In

The World's Great Religions

LIFE's Picture History of Western Man

The LIFE Treasury of American Folklore

America's Arts and Skills

The Second World War

LIFE's Picture History of World War II

Picture Cook Book

LIFE Guide to Paris

THE
GLORY
OF
CHRISTMAS

BY THE EDITORS OF
LIFE

A
STONEHENGE
BOOK

TIME INCORPORATED, NEW YORK

TIME INC. BOOK DIVISION

Editor Norman P. Ross

Copy Director William Jay Gold   *Art Director* Edward A. Hamilton

Chief of Research Beatrice T. Dobie

Editorial staff for Volume One of
THE LIFE BOOK OF CHRISTMAS

Editor Stanley Fillmore

Designer Kenneth Hine

Text John Stanton

Chief Researcher Carlotta Kerwin

Researchers Audrey Foote, Mary Ellen Murphy, Kaye Neil,
Donald Nelson, Jean Sulzberger

Picture Researchers Margaret K. Goldsmith, Joan T. Lynch, Sue Bond

Art Associate Robert L. Young

Art Assistants James D. Smith, John Newcomb,
Robert McElrath, David Wyland

Copy Staff Marian Gordon Goldman,
Rosalind Stubenberg, Dolores A. Littles

Publisher Jerome S. Hardy

General Manager John A. Watters

LIFE MAGAZINE

Editor Edward K. Thompson

Managing Editor George P. Hunt

Publisher C. D. Jackson

The following individuals and departments of Time
Inc. helped in producing this book: Dmitri Kessel,
LIFE staff photographer; Doris O'Neil, Chief of the
LIFE Picture Library; Content Peckham, Chief of
the Time Inc. Bureau of Editorial Reference; Donald
Bermingham and Clara Applegate of the TIME-LIFE
News Service; Correspondents Gerda Endler (Bonn),
Marlin Levin (Jerusalem), Katharine Sachs (Lon-
don), Piero Saporiti (Madrid), Page d'Aulnay and
Joseph Harriss (Paris), Gertraud Lessing (Vienna).

CONTENTS
VOLUME ONE

INTRODUCTION

The story of Jesus' birth and of the momentous events of His life was first related by the four Evangelists, who are depicted on the opposite page composing their gospels. At upper left, St. Matthew appears to be pausing in his work to listen to inspirational advice from the angel, the symbol traditionally associated with him. St. Mark, at upper right, turns his head toward the lion, which is his sign. At lower left, St. Luke, attended by the ox, his symbol, is portrayed in deep contemplation. St. John, seen at lower right with his symbolic eagle, is dipping his quill. The stylized portraits of these saints illuminate a gospel book created for the Emperor Charlemagne in the Eighth Century.

Since Charlemagne's artists decorated their New Testament manuscripts, books without end have been written about Christmas. There have been books of great art on the subject of Christmas; books on Christmas traditions; books of stories with a Christmas background; collections of Christmas music; books of recipes and instructions for decorating in the Christmas spirit; and anthologies, not necessarily *about* Christmas, put together *for* the Christmas season. But no single work exists that brings together the best aspects of all these various books. THE LIFE BOOK OF CHRISTMAS is designed to fill this gap.

Photographers, reporters and researchers, advised by scholars and art historians, searched through the world's great churches, museums and libraries for paintings, literature, sculpture, music, illuminated manuscripts and altarpieces. And they received, in the spirit of Christmas, unexpected gifts from strangers who heard of the book and contributed their favorite Christmas songs and stories.

THE LIFE BOOK OF CHRISTMAS comprises three volumes. This, the first volume, recounts the glory of the Nativity and its fulfillment in terms of Christ's life and His Resurrection. Each of the book's eight chapters begins with a scriptural passage that introduces the subject. The quotations are taken from the King James version of the Bible because it is so familiar and so revered for its literary quality. Then, in text and reproductions of master paintings and sculpture, the chapters explore the first Christmas, illuminating the lives and times of the participants, tracing the legends (like those of the Three Kings) and the traditions (such as the crèche) that have grown up around the Biblical accounts. The chapters end with an anthology of text and music that sheds additional light on the chapter. These selections come from many sources: historical documents; church music and popular carols; the works of writers great and obscure; the interpretations of scholars and theologians. They also include excerpts from apocryphal texts.

Volume Two traces the vivid pageantry of Christmas customs and celebrations since early Christian times. And Volume Three is a compilation of recipes for Christmas food and drink, and instructions for making Christmas decorations and for playing the traditional Christmas games.

—THE EDITORS OF LIFE

I

THE PROPHECIES

AND THERE SHALL COME FORTH a rod out of the stem of Jesse, and a Branch shall grow out of his roots: And the spirit of the Lord shall rest upon him, the spirit of wisdom and understanding, the spirit of counsel and might, the spirit of knowledge and of the fear of the Lord; And shall make him of quick understanding in the fear of the Lord: and he shall not judge after the sight of his eyes, neither reprove after the hearing of his ears: But with righteousness shall he judge the poor, and reprove with equity for the meek of the earth: and he shall smite the earth with the rod of his mouth, and with the breath of his lips shall he slay the wicked. . . . The voice of him that crieth in the wilderness, Prepare ye the way of the Lord, make straight in the desert a highway for our God. ISAIAH, 11:1-4; 40:3

ISAIAH, *whose eloquent voice predicted the coming of Christ, is shown here idealized in baroque grandeur in a German church.*

EXALTED VISION
OF A
MESSIAH
IN THE
HOLY LAND

A 13TH CENTURY PSALTER *from England includes this version of the tree of Jesse with a border decorated with Scriptural scenes.*

GOD'S WORDS were carried to mankind by His servants, the prophets. The prophets who wrote the exalted verses of the Book of Isaiah opening this volume were not the only ones to foretell the coming of a Messiah.

For centuries, the prophets had held before the Hebrews the hope of the coming of an era of holiness and union with God—the "Kingdom of God," as it came to be known—when sin and evil would be destroyed. Israel, the chosen, would be the first to be brought into that kingdom, which from Israel would then spread out until it embraced all the nations of the earth.

At first, the Hebrews looked to the royal family of David, rather than to any one king of the Davidic line, as the earthly agent through which God would set up His kingdom among men. But as king after

king disappointed the expectation of the people, the vision of the prophets turned to one anointed king of David's house, the Messiah, the king of the "End of Days" through whom God would finally and for all time establish the awaited kingdom.

Daniel cried: "I saw in the night visions, and, behold, one like the Son of man came with the clouds of heaven, and came to the Ancient of days, and they brought him near before him. And there was given him dominion, and glory, and a kingdom, that all people, nations, and languages should serve him: his dominion is an everlasting dominion, which shall not pass away, and his kingdom that which shall not be destroyed." And many others—Micah, Jeremiah, Ezekiel, Zechariah, Malachi—said much the same.

As the first Christmas drew near, the people of Israel were held captive once more, this time by the Romans, whose evil agent was Herod. The people yearned for a redeemer who would, they felt sure, deliver them from their tormentor.

In a village just west of Jerusalem, a boy named John was growing up who would soon go into the wilderness to baptize and prepare the people for the coming of the Lord. The land of Canaan stood expectant.

And what was Canaan? A little country of long vistas, tawny colors, delicately molded mountains and a dry, shining light in which to see it all. It was a country for contemplation, a timeless place that invited thoughts on eternity. A man could

stroll its length in a week, walk its breadth in a few days and come to know and love every tree and rock in it, for it stretched only 165 miles, most of it along the eastern shore of the Mediterranean, and reached inland not more than 87 miles.

Behind the sun-washed beaches were fertile plains where grain, vegetables, olives, figs and grapes grew. Eastward, behind the plains, rose mountains intersected by deep gorges and valleys.

This was The Land and in it lived perhaps a half million Jews. Elsewhere in the Roman Empire, some two million more Jews lived and many of them made yearly pilgrimages to Jerusalem, especially at Passover time. Those Jews who lived in the Holy Land were sometimes merchants, rich landowners or skilled craftsmen. But most were farmers and herdsmen. They were proud that King David had been a shepherd and the prophet Amos a "dresser of sycamore trees."

Wherever a Jew turned in this land he found monuments to the splendor of his past. Each holy well, sacred mountain and battlefield was part of the rich tapestry of his history. Scattered about were places which soon would take on new importance: Nazareth, a village so small it is not mentioned in the Old Testament; Bethlehem, a sleepy little herders' town; and Jerusalem—majestic Jerusalem—a city which even on the eve of that first Christmas possessed a thousand years of religious tradition as the city of David and the site of the Temple of Solomon.

THE FAMILY TREE *of Jesus in the 13th Century French Psalter of Inge-borg (left) starts with Jesse, reclining at bottom. His line includes David with his "vièle," Solomon with his harp, the Virgin Mary, and Jesus at the top. In descending order at left are prophets Malachi, Daniel and Amos, each bearing his prophecy of the Messiah, and on the right, a sibyl; Ezekiel; and Aaron, brother of Moses and the first high priest of the Jews.*

THE VILLAGE OF PEKI'IN *is said, by long tradition, to be the oldest Holy Land community continuou*

A LIFE
OF
VILLAGE WAYS

Most people of the Holy Land lived in little hamlets such as Nazareth or Peki'in, an Upper Galilean village shown above. Those villagers would not feel much out of place should they be returned through time to their former homes. For much of the countryside and many of the small villages remain largely unchanged.

By day the villagers tended farms. By night they rested on their rooftops. And a boy not yet born would later teach: "What ye hear in the ear that preach ye upon the housetops."

habited by Jews. Its houses go back only 200 years, but the carob trees (left center) appeared miraculously, legends say, 1,800 years ago.

HOLY LAND SITES *on the map are Jaffa, from which Jonah sailed; Caesarea, Herod's capital; Bethlehem, where Jesus would be born; Nazareth, where He would grow up; Jericho, near the place of His baptism; Capernaum, where He was to teach; Jerusalem, where He would die and rise again.*

13

PLACID AND SERENE *is the Sea of Galilee,*
then as now known as the Sea of Kinneret,
meaning harp-shaped. Here once lived
four boys who would later become Apostles.

ALONG
QUIET SHORES
OF SEAS
MADE HOLY

Everywhere the waters of the Holy Land evoke the majestic dramas that were long ago played out along their banks. The shores of the Dead Sea *(left)* in the shadowy days of antiquity cradled five "cities of the plain." Two of them had fallen into vile sin, and as Genesis reports: "Then the Lord rained upon Sodom and Gomorrah brimstone and fire. . . ." And near the Dead Sea's shores lived the community of Essene ascetics whose collected writings today are providing new insight into pre-Christian tenets.

Upstream from the Dead Sea, via the winding River Jordan, crossed in their wanderings so many times by the tribes of Israel, was the Sea of Kinneret *(above),* which is really a lake 13 miles long by 6 wide. Its waters are calm, with lake breezes that can turn into sudden storms, buffeting boats about. It teemed with fish. By the time of that first Christmas it was ringed by more settlements than are there today. These villages were full of fishermen and fish picklers. And to one of these hamlets, Capernaum, the boy who would be born in Bethlehem and grow up in Nazareth would come as a grown man. On the hillside and on such shores as the one shown above, He would begin to preach a divine mission that has never ended.

SULLEN AND OPPRESSIVE *are the gravelly shores of the Dead Sea. Pilings mark the site of an*
old potash works. No fish can live in these waters, five times saltier than those of the ocean.

SNOW-TOPPED SLOPES *of Mount Hermon (above) brood on fields of trees and grain. Legend says Hermon's jealous tears, when God met Moses on Mount Sinai, created the River Jordan.*

THE LAND
OF
SACRED LEGEND

This land, this speck in the immensities of the Roman Empire came to haunt the minds of many peoples. A place of barren cliffs, luxuriant valleys, deep defiles and a view of snow-capped peaks, The Land was about to become more: a treasure house sparkling with the truths of the world's yesterdays. In another time the American Negro, caught by holy mysteries, would hauntingly sing, "Oh, way o-ver Jor-dan, view the land, view the land; Way o-ver Jor-dan go view the heav'nly land."

STEEP SLOPES *of the Dishon defile (below) are the corroded product of the small brook at the bottom. This is the land where Barak lived and from here he marched to smite the Canaanites.*

STONY SLOPE *of a hillock near Nazareth (opposite) is where townsmen tried to kill Jesus for chiding them for lacking faith in Him.*

THE OLD, OLD WAR *of man against camel is renewed in a narrow cobblestone street of Bethlehem where an Arab pleads with a beast, loaded with green olive branches, to take one more step.*

THE SONS
OF THE EARTH

The days of the Holy Land went by slowly, so the minutes and hours were ignored. Then, as even now, patient drivers wailed their age-old beseeching cry to the stubborn camel, and in the fields shepherds, young and old alike, guarded their flocks against hyenas, wolves and jackals that roamed the country. Theirs was the basic pastoral life of the Holy Land of old.

The boy who would be born in Bethlehem would watch the shep-herds and later, in His mature years, would teach in their images. He would speak of the difficulty of get-ting camels and rich men through narrow places. And He would speak of the Good Shepherd whose sheep loved him, knew his voice and fol-lowed him. He would describe the joy in heaven over a repentant sinner in terms of the joy in a shepherd's heart over the return of a lost sheep. For these were symbols every man in Israel knew and could understand.

THE OLD VIGIL *over the flocks is carried on today near Bethlehem in the same way it was when David tended his sheep on these fields. And David would not have been dressed much differently.*

THE PROPHETS

What manner of men were they who foretold events of the future? Was their prophecy human or divine? Dr. Abraham J. Heschel, an eminent Jewish theologian, explores such questions in "The Prophets" (1962). This excerpt summarizes his thought-provoking answers.

As a witness, the prophet is more than a messenger. As a messenger, his task is to deliver the word; as a witness, he must bear testimony that the word is divine.

The words the prophet utters are not offered as souvenirs. His speech to the people is not a reminiscence, a report, hearsay. The prophet not only conveys; he reveals. He almost does unto others what God does unto him. In speaking, the prophet reveals God. This is the marvel of a prophet's work: in his words, *the invisible God becomes audible.* He does not prove or argue. The thought he has to convey is more than language can contain. Divine power bursts in the words. The authority of the prophet is in the Presence his words reveal.

CRADLE OF THE KINGDOM

Nazareth, home of Joseph and Mary and the town where Jesus grew to manhood, long has attracted writers and artists. This excerpt from "The Life of Jesus," by the noted 19th Century French philosopher Ernest Renan, not only pictures the town and its people but relates them in understandable, contemporary terms to the countryside Jesus came to know and love so well.

Nazareth was a small town in a hollow opening broadly at the summit of the group of mountains which close the plain of Esdraelon on the north. The population is now from three to four thousand, and it can never have varied much. The cold there is sharp in winter, and the climate very healthy. The town, like all the small Jewish towns at this period, was a heap of huts built without style, and would exhibit that harsh and poor aspect which villages in Semitic countries now present. The houses, it seems, did not differ much from those cubes of stone, without exterior or interior elegance, which still cover the richest parts of the Lebanon, and which, surrounded with vines and fig-trees, are still very agreeable. The environs, moreover, are charming; and no place in the world was so well adapted for dreams of perfect happiness. Even in our times Nazareth is still a delightful abode, the only place, perhaps, in Palestine in which the mind feels itself relieved from the burden which oppresses it in this unequaled desolation. The people are amiable and cheerful; the gardens fresh and green. Anthony the Martyr, at the end of the sixth century, drew an enchanting picture of the fertility of the environs, which he compared to paradise. Some valleys on the western side fully justify his description. The fountain, where formerly the life and gaiety of the little town were concentrated, is destroyed; its broken channels contain now only a muddy stream. But the beauty of the women who meet there in the evening—that beauty which was remarked even in the sixth century, and which was looked upon as a gift of the Virgin Mary—is still most strikingly preserved. It is the Syrian type in all its languid grace. No doubt Mary was there almost every day, and took her place with her jar on her shoulder in the file of her companions who have remained unknown. . . . .

The horizon from the town is limited. But if we ascend a little the plateau, swept by a perpetual breeze, which overlooks the highest houses, the prospect is splendid. On the west are seen the fine outlines of Carmel, terminated by an abrupt point which seems to plunge into the sea. Before us are spread out the double summit which towers above Megiddo; the mountains of the country of Schechem, with their holy places of the patriarchal age; the hills of Gilboa, the small, picturesque group to which are attached the graceful or terrible recollections of Shunem and of Endor; and Tabor, with its beautiful rounded form, which antiquity compared to a bosom. Through a depression between the mountains of Shunem and Tabor are seen the valley of the Jordan and the high plains of Paræa, which form a continuous line from the eastern side. On the north, the mountains of Safed, in inclining toward the sea conceal St. Jean d'Acre, but permit the Gulf of Khaïfa to be distinguished. Such was the horizon of Jesus. This enchanted circle, cradle of the kingdom of God, was for years his world. Even in his later life he departed but little beyond the familiar limits of his childhood. For yonder, northward, a glimpse is caught, almost on the flank of Hermon, of Cæsarea-Philippi, his furthest point of advance into the Gentile world; and here southward, the more sombre aspect of these Samaritan hills foreshadows the dreariness of Judea beyond, parched as by a scorching wind of desolation and death.

If the world, remaining Christian, but attaining to a better idea of the esteem in which the origin of its religion should be held, should ever wish to replace by authentic holy places the mean and apocryphal sanctuaries to which the piety of dark ages attached itself, it is upon this height of Nazareth that it will rebuild its temple. There, at the birthplace of Christianity, and in the centre of the actions of its Founder, the great church ought to be raised in which all Christians may worship. There, also, on this spot where sleep Joseph, the carpenter, and thousands of forgotten Nazarenes who never passed beyond the horizon of their valley, would be a better station than any in the world beside for the philosopher to contemplate the course of human affairs, to console himself for their uncertainty, and to reassure himself as to the Divine end which the world pursues through countless falterings. . . .

ECLOGUE IV

Not only the Bible spoke of the coming of a heavenly child. The Roman poet Vergil did so in the poem below, written some 30 years before Jesus' birth. Probably it referred to the heir desired by a noble family, but in the Middle Ages it was taken as a Messianic prophecy.

The last great age, foretold by sacred rimes,
Renews its finished course: Saturnian times
Roll round again; and mighty years, begun
From their first orb, in radiant circles run.
The base degen'rate iron offspring ends;
A golden progeny from heav'n descends.
O chaste Lucina! speed the mother's pains;
And haste the glorious birth!

Jerusalem Gaude

The exultant words of the prophet Zechariah are sung in Seventh Century Gregorian chant at Vespers on "Gaudete" (Rejoice) Sunday in some church liturgies. This service occurs on the second Sunday before Christmas.

Je - ru - sa - lem re - joice, be glad and joy - ful, for__ there__ shall__ come__ un - to thee a Sav - ior, al - le - lu - ia.

II

THE ANNUNCIATION

AND IN THE SIXTH MONTH THE angel Gabriel was sent from God unto a city of Galilee, named Nazareth, To a virgin espoused to a man whose name was Joseph, of the house of David; and the virgin's name was Mary. And the angel came in unto her, and said, Hail, thou that art highly favoured, the Lord is with thee: blessed art thou among women. And when she saw him, she was troubled at his saying, and cast in her mind what manner of salutation this should be. And the angel said unto her, Fear not, Mary: for thou hast found favour with God. And, behold, thou shalt conceive in thy womb, and bring forth a son, and shalt call his name Jesus.... And Mary said, Behold the handmaid of the Lord; be it unto me according to thy word. And the angel departed from her. LUKE, 1:26-31, 38

GENTLE VIRGIN *is depicted by Rogier van der Weyden in a detail from the 15th Century Columba altarpiece, now in Munich.*

SIMPLE WORDS,
A COMPLEX
MESSAGE

MARY'S HUMILITY *in the presence of God's messenger is mixed with surprise in this illumination from a 15th Century manuscript.*

TERTULLIAN, one of the early Church fathers, writing of the religious significance of the Annunciation, said: "Eve believed the serpent, Mary believed Gabriel; the one sinned by believing, the other by believing effaced the sin."

Luke, whose unadorned narrative of this supreme event opens this chapter, and the angel Gabriel shared an important talent: In delivering a message, each knew which details to emphasize, which to leave out. The message that Gabriel brought to the Virgin—that she was to "conceive . . . and bring forth a son, and . . . call his name Jesus"—is a message that brought her joy, grief and glory. But Gabriel wasted no words. He left it to Mary's faith, to her intelligence and imagination, to supply the details that he left out. And Mary was equal to the test.

The message that Luke related —the account of the angel Gabriel's Annunciation to Mary—changed the world for all time. But Luke also wasted no words. He concentrated on the essentials and left it to his readers to interpret the message in the light of their faith. Theologians and artists through the ages have accepted Luke's implied invitation and have used his chronicle as the

source of inspirations that have enriched the whole of Christendom.

The Annunciation is the beginning of the Christmas story. Theologians assume that the Incarnation —the assumption of human flesh by God in the person of Christ—took place the moment that Mary freely accepted her role by saying to Gabriel: "Be it unto me according to thy word." Thus it is that the Feast of the Annunciation is celebrated March 25, just nine months before Christmas.

Luke's chronicle and the account given from Joseph's viewpoint beginning at Matthew 1:18 are the bases for the doctrine of the Virgin Birth. That doctrine, first authoritatively stated about 150 A.D., is included in both the Nicene and Apostles' Creeds and is held as an article of faith by Roman Catholic and Eastern Orthodox communicants. Beginning in the 19th Century some Protestant liberals rejected the doctrine. However, many Protestants hold to the belief.

On these pages, paintings show Mary and Gabriel in a variety of poses, locales and moods. The very differences point up the universality of Luke's words, the only scriptural account of the Annunciation to Mary. Because Luke set no strictures to restrain them, artists have been free to depict the Annunciation in terms that were both theologically and artistically suited to their civilizations. And, borrowing from apocryphal sources, they developed a rich symbolism that lent deep meaning to their art.

One of the major differences in paintings over the ages is in the status of Mary in relation to Gabriel. In the earliest works, the frescoes of the catacombs of Priscilla in Rome,

the Virgin is seated, as though overwhelmed by the news. This is true, also, of works from the early medieval period in which Mary is depicted as humble and submissive. Gabriel, glorious in his kingly robes and carrying a scepter, is the main figure.

After the 14th Century, Mary generally is dominant and the angel is sometimes shown kneeling to her and carrying the lily, her symbol, rather than his own scepter. The change has been attributed to the works of St. Bonaventure, the source of many traditions in Italian art. St. Bonaventure was probably reflecting a growing emphasis in the Church on Mary's exalted position. In other early paintings the Virgin often is depicted as spinning wool and in later paintings as reading holy books.

Luke said nothing about the setting of the scene. Early painters usually placed it in a vaguely defined temple or house, or in a garden patio as in the painting at right. About the same time that Fra Angelico was painting his Annunciation in the early part of the 15th Century, however, a Flemish master believed to be Robert Campin did the famous Merode Altarpiece which is shown on the following pages. This is an early example of a new trend in detailed and realistic interpretation of the Annunciation to Mary in a domestic setting.

The Merode also summarized the learning of centuries in its superb use of symbolism. In the Fra Angelico, for example, the Incarnation is represented by the dove. But in the Merode, each household item holds a symbolic meaning, so that the entire work is permeated with rich allusions to the life of Christ.

GABRIEL'S ANNUNCIATION *is written on this fresco in two lines of Latin, and Mary's answer in one inverted line in between. The Adam and Eve scene (background) is a reminder of original sin, which Jesus will come to expiate. Fra Angelico painted this work about 1430.*

HOLY SIGNS
IN
HOMELY THINGS

The Merode Altarpiece is a triptych, a painting done in three separate panels but meant to be viewed as a single work. It depicts one of the most dramatic moments of the Annunciation, as Mary, unaware of the angel's presence, unaware of the spirit of God, goes on reading. Except for the presence of the angel, the scene might be in any 15th Century Flemish household. But the work is a tour de force of symbolic meaning.

For more than five centuries experts have studied the painting and have read symbolic meanings into many of the commonplace items depicted. In the left panel, the rosebush symbolizes the Crucifixion; the open door, hope; the key represents desire for God. In the center panel, the water basin above Gabriel and the towel beside it signify Mary's purity and cleanliness. Joseph, in his shop in the right panel, is working on a foot warmer or possibly on a spike-board such as the one tied to Jesus on His way to Calvary. In the left panel, the kneeling figures most likely portray the pious donor of the painting and his wife or betrothed.

EXOTIC OR COMMON, ALL THINGS SPEAK OF JESUS

CHRIST'S ENTRY *into the world carrying the Cross symbolizes His Incarnation and Crucifixion.*

A MOUSETRAP *on Joseph's bench alludes to the concept that Christ's sacrifice trapped the devil.*

The richness of the scholarship and imagination of the painter (considered by many art experts to have been Robert Campin) have made the Merode Altarpiece a source of fascination for more than 500 years. Through the use of traditional symbols and his own creations, he infused the painting with a sense of God's presence. Some of the painted metaphors are obvious, some deep and involved.

The traditional symbol for the Incarnation is the presence of the dove of the Holy Ghost. In the Merode detail at top left, Campin painted the Christ Child gliding toward the Virgin on a beam of light that represents the light of God. The passage of the figure through the closed window recalls the comment by St. Bernard on the Virgin Birth that, just as the sun penetrates a glass window without damaging it, "thus the Word of God, the splendor of the Father, entered the virgin chamber and then came forth from the closed womb." The mousetrap at bottom left gives the work its popular title, "The Madonna of the Mousetrap." The trap alludes to a concept of St. Augustine that the human form of Christ fooled the devil as bait fools a mouse. The trap that caught the devil and atoned for the sin of man was the Crucifixion. The tools are emblems of Joseph. The lilies in the pitcher *(opposite)* represent the Virgin's purity. Because a lighted candle symbolizes Christ's divinity, the extinguished candle puzzles scholars. Some hold that the painter meant to show that in the lowly state Christ assumed at the Incarnation, His divinity was concealed by His human form. Another view holds that divine radiance snuffed out the candle.

SYMBOLIC LILIES *suggest Mary's purity. Scholars differ on the meaning of the burned-out candle.*

ON THE ANNUNCIATION OF FRA ANGELICO

As the Annunciation has inspired artists, so their work has moved poets. The painting on page 25 drew from Spain's Manuel Machado (1874-1947) this tribute to the artist.

The silver carolling of Matins woke
  The angel artist from his couch to paint,
  While round him throng a rosy chorus quaint
Of cherubs waiting on his brush's stroke.

They guide his hand to set the snowy light
  On Mary's brow and o'er her lovely cheeks
  To show the eyes wherein her pureness speaks,
To limn her slender fingers amber white.

Their angel wings unto his eyes they hold
  So he may copy of their child-like snows
The plumes of him who brought her message here;
  Who rays amid his pearly vestment stoled,
  His light upon the Virgin's breast of rose,
Like vivid sunburst on some crystal sphere.

The Annunciation in Flanders

A compassionate approach to the Annunciation tableau is found in "The Christ Child in Flanders," a retelling of the story by Felix Timmermans (1886-1927). With poetic license but no loss of reverence, the tale unfolds against the background of Flanders in the Middle Ages.

Mary stopped. Glancing up from her heavy breviary, she saw that the sharp sickle of the moon was already hanging in the mother-of-pearl heavens. . . .

Mary buried her nose in the yellow flowers she had arranged in the blue Delft vase on the table and sighed. Delicious longing flooded her heart, making her sit very still and close her eyes. It was the womanly desire to have children, dear gentle children with blonde hair and ruddy cheeks, who in her girlish fancy never grew up, and who would be given her as dew is given the evening meadows.

Mary turned from the window with a sigh. Throwing her blue calico cloak about her shoulders, she took her prayerbook from the mantel and set out to church. As she strode down the birch path her skirts rustled in the stillness.

Then it happened.

Sweetest music blew through the delicate twigs of the birches. Startled, Mary looked up, and when her gaze fell back to the path in front of her, there, woven of evening mists and moonlight, stood an angel of marvelous beauty dressed in cherry-red vestments, a lily in his hand.

Heavenly fire blazed through him, and he glowed like a cathedral window in the sun. With a rush of huge dove's wings he lifted himself from the ground, and an overpowering fragrance as of violets and cloves emanated from him.

It was as though Mary suddenly stood face to face with all she had longed for and been unable to express. Unafraid (though not daring to look into the angel's face) and melting with reverence and humility, she knelt down in the dog-daisies of the path.

Wondrously sweet as no sound ever before heard by human ear, from the throat of the magnificent angel, as though from organ-pipes, rang words of greeting, the message that she was to carry the Lord and was of all women the most blessed, she and the holy fruit of her womb.

Mary dared not ask how this would come about, but the angel sang on: "The Holy Spirit will come upon thee, and the power of the Most High will overshadow thee." There was a silence. Into it, in complete surrender and trembling with happiness, Mary replied: "Behold the handmaid of the Lord; let it be unto me according to thy word." When she raised her head to thank the angel with her eyes, the music faded out of the trees, and there was silence again and evening loneliness, and a heavy fog covering the fields.

When Mary reached the house she forgot to light the lamp and sank weeping upon the table. She wept from an overwhelming joy and the strangeness of her blessing, her tears falling on the yellow flowers.

Outside the heavens stood full of stars.

ANNUNCIATION TO MARY

German writer Rainer Maria Rilke (1875-1926), one of the great modern poets, had a mystical view of God. His fervor shines through this re-creation of the poignant moment when Mary fully realized the presence of the angel.

Not that an angel entered (mark this)
was she startled. Little as others start
when a ray of sun or the moon by night
busies itself about their room,
would she have been disturbed by the shape
in which an angel went;
she scarcely guessed that this sojourn
is irksome for angels. (O if we knew
how pure she was. Did not a hind, that,
recumbent, once espied her in the wood,
so lose itself in looking, that in it,
quite without pairing, the unicorn begot itself,
the creature of light, the pure creature—.)
Not that he entered, but that he,
the angel, so bent close to her
a youth's face that his gaze and that
with which she looked up struck together,
as though outside it were suddenly all empty
and what millions saw, did, bore,
were crowded into them: just she and he;
seeing and what is seen, eye and eye's delight
nowhere else save at this spot—: lo,
this is startling. And they were startled both.

Then the angel sang his melody.

The Angel Gabriel

The carol "Gabriel's Message" (below) was originally written in Basque, or Euzkara, an ancient tongue still spoken in parts of northern Spain and southern France.

The an-gel Ga-bri-el from hea-ven came___, His wings as drifted snow, his eyes___ as flame; "All hail," said he, "thou low-ly maid-en Ma-ry___, Most high-ly fa-vored la-dy," Glo - - - - - - ri - a!

III

THE BLESSED BIRTH

AND IT CAME TO PASS IN THOSE days, that there went out a decree from Caesar Augustus, that all the world should be taxed. (And this taxing was first made when Cyrenius was governor of Syria.) And all went to be taxed, every one into his own city. And Joseph also went up from Galilee, out of the city of Nazareth, into Judaea, unto the city of David, which is called Bethlehem; (because he was of the house and lineage of David:) To be taxed with Mary his espoused wife, being great with child. And so it was, that, while they were there, the days were accomplished that she should be delivered. And she brought forth her firstborn son, and wrapped him in swaddling clothes, and laid him in a manger; because there was no room for them in the inn. LUKE, 2:1-7

A LOVING MOTHER, *Mary attends to Jesus.*
This relief is at Chartres Cathedral, which
was built to her glory in the 13th Century.

BETHLEHEM'S HOUR
OF GLORY

GOD'S RADIANCE *pours down on the Nativity scene at Bethlehem in this delicate miniature from a 15th Century Book of Hours.*

A SIMPLE WOMAN goes on a journey with her husband and, while away from home, gives birth to a baby boy. This is the story, an ordinary story, that Luke sets forth in the plain verses on the preceding page. They tell of no miracles, make no demands on faith. And yet this birth is Christmas.

All the midnight masses, vesper services, clouds of drifting incense, choirs chanting in vaulted cathedrals, prayers arising from Christians of all persuasions and races on all the world's continents—all these celebrate Christmas. And so does all the bustling, warmhearted, pagan-tinged merriment: the gathering of the families, the decorating of the houses, the feasts and the gift-giving.

In the shadows, biding their time at this season of the year, stand those who would quarrel with Luke's account. They argue that Jesus was born at Nazareth, His parents' home, for there would be no reason for a tiring journey at this time.

The dissenters argue thus: Luke says—and no one questions—that

Jesus was born during Herod's reign. The saint further says that the reason for Mary and Joseph's journey to Bethlehem was to comply with an order by Cyrenius, the governor of Syria, to register for a census in the village of one's forebears. But, point out the dissidents, these two statements do not make sense: Herod died in 4 B.C. Thus, Jesus must have been born before then. Yet Cyrenius did not order the census until sometime between 6 and 9 A.D.

Luke altered fact, say skeptical scholars, to make Jesus' birth conform to the prophecy of Micah: " . . . thou, Bethlehem Ephratah . . . out of thee shall he come forth unto me that is to be ruler in Israel."

Yet other learned men agree with Luke. There is evidence, they suggest, that Cyrenius served two terms as governor and could well have presided over an earlier census—now forgotten—taken about 6 B.C., Jesus' probable birth year, during the final years of Herod's life.

Luke's account of the Birth is couched in the simplest of words: "And she brought forth her first-born son, and wrapped him in swaddling clothes, and laid him in a manger, because there was no room for them in the inn." Daniel-Rops, the eminent contemporary French writer, says in *Jesus and His Times,* "It is futile to attempt to embroider this plain statement." Yet the embroidery has gone on for centuries and still proceeds. The version which follows is almost pure speculation; no one can vouch for more than Luke reveals. Yet in their hearts, most Christians follow Mary and Joseph on their time-hallowed journey over the plains and hills.

In all probability, their route took them 90 miles from Nazareth to Jerusalem where, as reverent Jews,

they would have visited the Temple, then six miles more to Bethlehem. It would take the holy pair—Mary, perhaps 16 years old and approaching the end of her pregnancy, and Joseph, middle-aged, slow-moving and thoughtful—about four days to complete the trip, but every step of it must have been of absorbing interest.

Down the tortuous road the holy couple moved, jostled by Jewish traders, Nabataean caravaneers, Babylonian merchants with gold rings in their noses. Mary and Joseph passed by Jacob's well, where, one day, Jesus would converse with the Samaritan woman. Then they came in sight of Jerusalem, with the Temple, rebuilt by Herod after it was plundered by Crassus and Pompey, the Temple that stirred the heart of every Jew.

In truth it was a crowded, noisy city through which Mary and Joseph pushed to the Temple. Streets were narrow and houses often blocked the way. Above the hubbub came the roars of soldiers leading some poor wretch, his cross on his back, to his crucifixion. Mary, great with child, made her way past places her Son would consecrate in His agony—Gethsemane, Golgotha.

Then at Bethlehem, Luke states, there was no room for them in the inn, signifying, possibly, that they needed more privacy than the open court of an oriental hospice could give them. They went up to one of the hillside caves used by shepherds to shelter their animals, and there the Child was born. Mary and Joseph, soon joined by others, knelt to adore Him. And in adoration of a different kind, artists, each in the style of his own country and his own time, would paint and repaint that scene. Some of their worshipful creations appear on the following pages.

ADORATION *of the Infant is presented in this unique view in a 15th Century manuscript illumination from "The Golden Legend" by Jacobus de Voragine. The Child, His parents, the ox and the ass are shown in a medieval European street, while in the fields outside the town the shepherds are shown approaching. Below are portrayed two tender and intimate scenes of Mary bathing and feeding the Babe as Joseph attends to chores.*

STERN AND ALOOF, *a Virgin, probably painted in the Seventh Century, gestures toward her Child. The picture, in Rome's Santa Maria Novella Church, was found under a later painting.*

MARY'S ALTERED ROLE IN CHRISTIANITY

After Mary had borne her Child, she wrapped Him in swaddling clothes and retired with Him to quiet places. We will see her again only fitfully: preparing her family for the flight into Egypt, worrying when the boy is lost in the Temple. She will be happy when He grants to her the miracle of the wine. She will understand when a voice from the crowd cries, "Blessed is the womb that bare thee and the paps which thou hast sucked," and He replies, "Yea rather, blessed are they that hear the word of God and keep it." She will stand and suffer by His Cross.

Once, in the joy of conception, she had sung "Yea, Behold, from henceforth all generations shall call me blessed." And this was so, although it was an austere blessedness, a cold and remote devotion that produced the Virgin in the picture above, sternly calling attention to the baby who is God. For this was the role the Church fathers first saw for her, a role of disciplinary firmness. It would take five centuries and the craving of generations for a merciful mediator at God's throne for mankind to recognize the Virgin's warmth and tenderness—qualities imbuing the statue opposite.

TENDER AND LOVING, *a Virgin and Child are sculpted in limestone over a door of Amiens Cathedral in France. Originally gilded, the statue now gleams goldenly in warm sunlight.*

THE INFANT MUSICIAN *is part of a complex representation of paradise by the 15th Century Master of the Upper Rhine. The walled garden is an old symbol of Mary's purity, derived from the "Song of Songs": "A garden inclosed is my sister, my spouse; a spring shut up, a fountain sealed."*

MOTHER
OF MERCY
AND HOPE

At services in all the great cathedrals, beloved hymns will resound again this Christmas season as they will in the village churches.

Carolers will softly sing, "Round yon Virgin mother and child, Holy Infant so tender and mild, sleep in heavenly peace." And many priests in ceremonial vestments will chant: "Mother of Jesus! Heaven's open gate, Star of the sea, support the fallen state of mortals, thou whose womb thy Maker bore; And yet, strange thing, a virgin, as before;

Who didst, from Gabriel's Hail, this news receive, Repenting sinners by thy prayers relieve."

For man, always a sinner, never felt his sinfulness more poignantly than he did in the Middle Ages. He felt that God was sublime, majestic, terrible, and there was no escaping from His stern justice, save perhaps through the intercession of a compassionate Mother.

The Middle Ages clung to her, and cathedral makers, sculptors, painters worked to her honor. Philoso-

phers sang her praises. Chaucer put Dante's words into his own tales: "Thow Mayde and Mooder, doghter of thy Sone Thow welle of mercy, synful soules cure."

Now the simple young woman of Nazareth was lost in the glittering world of art. With the Reformation, her exaltation diminished as many Protestant and Catholic theologians opposed elevating her to godhood. But already Mary had touched the depth of millions, and devotion to her became a never-ending well.

ENTHRONED IN A CHURCH, *Mother and Child are depicted by Jan van Eyck in an architectural setting almost humorously remote from those in which Mary and Jesus lived their days.*

A NEW MEXICAN MADONNA *holding her Child dates from the 19th Century. Their attire and skin tones suggest Indian influences.*

AN AFRICAN MADONNA, *attending to her chores with her Child on her back, is the work of a pupil in a modern African school.*

THE VIRGIN IN ALL PARTS OF THE WORLD

With the passing centuries, devotion to the Blessed Virgin spread throughout the world. She became universal and varied. She was dark in Italy, fair-haired in Holland, thin in Spain and plump in France. In Mexico she was an Aztec maiden, the Virgin of Guadalupe, but she was also another, the Virgin of los Remedios, for the Spaniards; and in Warsaw she was a Polish woman. Chinese artists made her an almond-eyed lady in flowing robes and placed her in Chinese setting—a moon gate, a pagoda and a lantern festival. Maori artists dressed her in long grass skirts. African carvers made her a Negro and put heavy coils of beads around her neck; sometimes they showed her as a simple worker, worn yet full of happy courage. Indian artists made her a high-caste Hindu sitting serenely by a stream.

Princes and marshals placed nations and armies under her protection. Crusaders clanked off to the Holy Land shouting her praises, patriot warriors of Poland rallied to her banners and sometimes great hosts hurled themselves on one another, both of them roaring for victory in the name of the Virgin. At Guadalupe in Mexico, at Lourdes in France, Fatima in Portugal and in other places, she is said to have appeared to mankind. And to the shrines in those places, the poor and sick and pious come to pray for her aid even today.

A CHINESE NATIVITY *is shown in a painting by Lu Hung Hien, who in 1941 was a student at* *the Catholic University of Peking. Missionaries were in China as early as the Seventh Century,* *but it was not until the period between the two world wars that a Chinese school of Christian* *art, hauntingly delicate and filled with a brooding peace, arose—and all too briefly flourished.*

FRANCIS' HOLY CUSTOM

At Greccio, Italy, in 1223, St. Francis of Assisi re-created the birth of Christ using life-size scenery, live actors, a wax figure of the Babe and living animals. Ever since, the crèche, or crib, has been a Christmas tradition. Sculptors, architects and painters have helped construct crèches, and

those built in such cities as Munich and Barcelona are noted for their ornate handiwork. But few equal the elaborateness of the one above, built for King Charles III of Naples in the 18th Century. Around Mary, Joseph and the Child clusters a busy Neapolitan world. While dining at an inn, a family on pilgrimage listens to a band. Porters lug the heavy trunks of the Magi, and over everyone hover cupids and elegant angels.

A Hymn on the Nativity of My Saviour

Ben Jonson, Elizabethan playwright (1572-1637), is firmly associated with Christmas chiefly because of the plays he wrote for court festivities. Here is his description of mankind's universal joy at the miracle of the Nativity.

I sing the birth was born to-night,
The Author both of life and light;
 The angels so did sound it,
And like the ravished shepherds said,
Who saw the light, and were afraid,
 Yet searched, and true they found it.

The Son of God, th' Eternal King,
That did us all salvation bring,
 And freed the soul from danger;
He whom the whole world could not take,
The Word, which heaven and earth did make;
 Was now laid in a manger.

The Father's wisdom willed it so,
The Son's obedience knew no No,
 Both wills were in one stature;
And as that wisdom had decreed,
The Word was now made Flesh indeed,
 And took on Him our nature.

What comfort by Him do we win,
Who made Himself the price of sin,
 To make us heirs of glory!
To see this Babe, all innocence,
A martyr born in our defence;
 Can man forget this story?

Joseph's Vision

Few versions of the Nativity story pay more than passing attention to Joseph. An exception is the Book of James, or Protevangelium, one of the New Testament apocryphal texts. In it appears this fragment, ostensibly in Joseph's words.

And I Joseph walked, and I walked not; and I looked up into the air, and saw the air violently agitated; and I looked up at the pole of heaven, and saw it stationary, and the fowls of heaven still; and I looked at the earth and saw a vessel lying, and workmen reclining by it, and their hands in the vessel, and those who handled did not handle it, and those who took did not lift, and those who presented it to their mouth did not present it, but the faces of all were looking up; and I saw the sheep scattered, and the sheep stood, and the shepherd lifted up his hand to strike them, and his hand remained up; and I looked at the stream of the river, and I saw that the mouths of the kids were down, and not drinking; and everything which was being impelled forward was intercepted in its course.

A Gothic Noel

Of the many elaborations on the Nativity story, few offer the blend of reverence, humor and imagination found in the tale condensed here. Written by Jehan Le Povremoyne, a contemporary French journalist and lecturer, it has been translated and adapted by Audrey Foote.

High above the drowsing village stands the Gothic cathedral, its spires pointing to the heavens. In the belltowers the wind murmurs an ancient and plaintive refrain as it did once upon a time over the stable of Bethlehem. The village, at peace beneath a clear night sky and the glittering stars, snuggles against its hillsides and goes to sleep.

At the cathedral, only St. Benoit is awake. He watches the lights die out in the twisted alleys where the antique signboards sway in the wind. He listens to the diminishing sounds of life in the town and the vanishing footsteps of vagrants returning from the taverns. And then, sure of not being seen by any human being, St. Benoit steps out of his niche by the grand portal and climbs the façade of the cathedral, hand over hand clinging to the rooted vines, until he reaches the tympan over the main doorway, where stand the sculptured figures of the Biblical prophets and martyrs.

"Noah? Isaiah? Abraham?"

He calls out, tugs at the hem of a mantle and with his stick prods the sleeping ones.

"Noah, it is I, Benoit, Brother Benoit."

"Brother Benoit?"

"Yes, from down below, from beside the little doorway."

"Ah yes; well, what do you wish, my brother?"

"I wanted to tell you, Noah, it is the eve of Noel. Noel, the feast of the redemption. The glorious Nativity on earth of the son of God. Noah?"

The mumble of his voice in his white beard is like a breeze in the forest of Ile de France. Amid the sculptured leaves and branches, allelulias seem to echo.

"Yes, Benoit," Noah answers, "I understand. I know. Let us give praise."

"No, not yet. Since Easter of the year 1426, I have been thinking over an idea which I wanted to confide to you. Tell me what you think of it."

And in the ear of Noah—an ear grey with ancient dust—St. Benoit confesses his great project. It must be something magnificent, fantastic, celestial and pious all at once; Noah, gay as the time he drank too much wine, kisses St. Benoit on both stony cheeks, cheeks eroded by the tears of the rain. At the tympan of the Old Testament they awaken the statues; the whole bizarre throng of Genesis, from Adam to Nathanael, arises.

And now they make their way along the exterior of the cathedral, along the balconies, under the flying buttresses; from time to time they pause and gaze down from the parapets on the sleeping village below. A rising murmur fills the towers, the spires, and vibrates against the stone roses from which the petals fall soundlessly on the parvis; the light folds of the virgins' draperies flutter.

"What is it?" all the Biblical figures whisper. "Why are you awakening us?"

All the saints of the New Testament now, the great saints from St. Martin to St. Louis, from the apostles to the most humble monks, have stepped out from their places. They are all different, no one is of the same size or height . . . there are large ones, lean in their long straight robes, little ones in their mantles and hoods. Some wear crowns, some miters . . . some are barefoot, others shod in the finest sandals; but they are all very old, very good, very holy—and very beautiful with all the beauty of Gothic sculpture.

And amid all this, St. Benoit continues to preach.

"My brothers, we are here to find the Holy Mother of God. So be it."

"So be it," they all mumble after him. "But what do you think of this, Chrysostome? A pretty sermon, but Benoit is making fun of us. Why does he waken us like this after so many centuries?"

But St. Benoit does not let himself be intimidated by either the kings or the people—far less by the clergy. Undaunted, he leads the crowd of saints toward the apse. For it is at the apse, high on the gable as on the prow of a ship, that the figure of the Virgin Mary stands, Our Lady of the Waves, for the protection of mariners. The saints press forward along the balconies, perch on the arches and on the lead roof; then from the throng arises an exquisite prayer towards the Madonna. Her hands joined, her head crowned, she steps forth from among the stars which sprinkle the velvety drapery of the sky; she listens to them and then smiles.

"Merciful Virgin, beautiful madonna," St. Benoit chants as the others chorus behind him.

"Queen! Queen of the angels!" the cherubs shout enthusiastically. . . .

St. Benoit speaks:

"Hail, Mary, full of grace. But the Saviour is not with you, and it is the eve of Noel. My brothers and I—we would be so happy if you would—"

"That Benoit, would you believe it," mutters St. Onesiphore. "What audacity!"

"If you would, Holy Mother, relive among us the fete of the Nativity."

A great silence falls on the cathedral; all are silent, holding their breath, listening.

"Relive the Nativity."

And in answer the Virgin steps down from her flowered pedestal. But St. Benoit stops her as she places one foot on the gutter. He is in command.

"This must be done properly," he says. "You must not go on foot, my lady, we—"

"We will carry you," volunteer the tiny angels who have but the tips of wings on their shoulders.

"Angels! will you do me the kindness of going off to play elsewhere? And just as fast as you can." St. Benoit climbs up on a broken buttress and then orders: "This way, Old Testament. All the Old Testament, by hierarchic order, naturally. But of course, Adam and Eve first. Please let them move up to the head of the line—the kings next. Then the prophets—hurry up, kings, will you please hurry up. There now, all the Old Testament marches in front. Yes, the angels can play their trumpets—but not too loudly! Don't play *yet*, angels! Wait a minute! O Holy Mother, what a lot of trouble!"

"Perhaps you would like your friends near you?" simpers St. Pacome.

"My friend," the Virgin says, "I wish only Joseph near to me—"

"Oh, St. Joseph!" exclaims St. Benoit. "I forgot all about St. Joseph! Where are you, Joseph? Joseph?"

The crowd of statues turns in search of the blessed carpenter. He is not to be found.

"St. Exupère, would you go and look for St. Joseph? Tell him that Madame the Virgin asks for him." St. Exupère and his cohorts go off.

"The New Testament will follow after Our Mother," Benoit commands. "The apostles first, yes, the apostles. St. Peter, stand there please, beside your brother. St. Paul—ah, but St. Paul, still preaching? You set a bad example! But no, look now, after the apostles come the martyrs. The popes? The popes? Will you Holinesses please be more cooperative! After the monks—yes, *after* them."

At this moment there is a stir in the crowd and St. Exupère emerges.

"Here is Joseph, long live St. Joseph," shout the saints. "Where was he?"

"Joseph thinks of everything. While we were here fussing futilely, he went to find the only mount which God has glorified on this earth—for the services which he rendered to the Mother and the Son. St. Joseph went to find—"

And the poor man of Nazareth steps aside; there stands a donkey. Alas, a very little donkey, from the tympan of the flight into Egypt; skinny, low slung, and missing ears and tail.

The Virgin smiles at her husband and then at the beast. With her beautiful fine hand of white stone, Our Lady strokes the worn little back; it is still solid enough in its carving, however, to carry the Madonna. And then with infinite precaution, for Mary suddenly feels herself heavy as on the day she left Nazareth, the maidens help her mount the blessed donkey.

St. Benoit, hoarse with emotion, announces:

"On route for the procession of Noel!"

Across the roofs of the old Gothic cathedral, among the marvelous stone lilies and vines, among the treasures worked by men who were artists and artists who were saints, the wonderful and droll procession of statues advances.

See them pass . . . across the luxuriant flora of stone flowers and rose windows and arabesques . . . down the stairways of the towers, advancing onto the large square before the cathedral where not even a dog scampers. The nave is soon filled, then the transepts, even the rood loft. The Virgin meanwhile has reached the chapel in the apse, *her* chapel.

On the steps of the high altar the Virgin reposes. Joseph, leaning on his staff, contemplates her, half smiling, half sad. To one side the little donkey kneels, and at the other an ox from the niche of St. Matthew, and all gaze upon the open space of blue and gold carpet where Jesus is to be born.

The throng of saints presses close to the screen of the choir which the beloved St. John has closed about his mother. The Old Testament and the New Testament await the Nativity. But just then St. Francis in his cowl approaches St. Benoit.

"My brother Benoit," he says. "It is not only mankind who should witness the Birth of Our Saviour. Our brothers the beasts would rejoice around the Virgin—"

And the Franciscans leave the cathedral, climb once more the pillars and the lintels, up to the highest and most hidden corners, and coax forth the fantastic fauna of the Middle Ages: horses, goats, hippocamps, crabs, scorpions, bulls and the beasts of the Apocalypse, all chiseled with love in the ateliers of the time of St. Louis. The animals descend, tumbling and leaping and cavorting, and under the guidance of the little Brothers, take their places in the majestic nave of the cathedral. The whole of the animal creation is there beside the ox and ass of Bethlehem: sheep, quail, piglets, lions, eagles and all the birds of the islands and the heavens, and all the fish of the oceans and all the creatures of the Gothic imagination.

All the sculptures of the cathedral are there, but alas, the Divine Infant does not descend. The angels sing in vain, St. Joseph struggles against drowsiness, the little donkey has cramps in his knees; all the little animals disport themselves like acrobats to divert the mother of God—but Jesus is not reborn.

But where is St. Benoit?

"Benoit? Benoit?" the saints whisper.

Benoit breaks through the crowd. Having put aside his cross and miter of abbé, Benoit lifts up on a fine folded cloth a beautiful smiling child, all glorious, with a globe of the world in one hand

and a royal crown on his brow. On both knees before the Virgin, Benoit speaks:

"Woman. Woman. Here is your son."

The saints are ecstatic, the apse glorious with supernatural light; the little animals twitter with ineffable joy in the torrent of grace, the Paradise, which descends upon them.

But suddenly a volley of bells shakes the cathedral. From the high belfries glistening in the dawn comes the rumble of the huge bells, howling like the ocean, into the overturned vessel where the saints of stone are praying.

"The angelus! The angelus!"

And the statues are immediately again on the roofs, the galleries, the towers, the tympans and the pillars, in their places of worldly immobility; and their escapade of an eve of Noel would never have been known to man had the poet not read in their ecstatic eyes the miraculous vision of which they dream now until the end of time.

The Rocking Carol

Lullabies sung to the heavenly baby—they are called "berceuses" in France and "Wiegenlieder" in Germany—send many an ordinary baby to sleep. The one below comes from an 18th Century Czech song, "Hajej, nynej, Ježíšku."

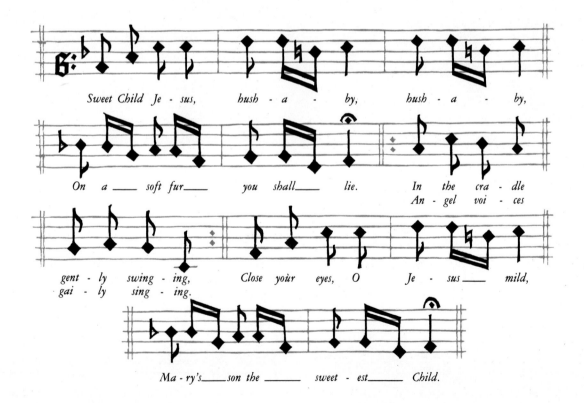

Sweet Child Je - sus, hush - a - by, hush - a - by,

On a soft fur you shall lie. In the cra - dle
An - gel voi - ces

gent - ly swing - ing, Close your eyes, O Je - sus mild,
gai - ly sing - ing.

Ma - ry's son the sweet - est Child.

IV

THE COURIERS OF GOD

AND THERE WERE IN THE SAME country shepherds abiding in the field, keeping watch over their flock by night. And, lo, the angel of the Lord came upon them, and the glory of the Lord shone round about them: and they were sore afraid. And the angel said unto them, Fear not: for, behold, I bring you good tidings of great joy, which shall be to all people. For unto you is born this day in the city of David a Saviour, which is Christ the Lord. And this shall be a sign unto you; Ye shall find the babe wrapped in swaddling clothes, lying in a manger. And suddenly there was with the angel a multitude of the heavenly host praising God, and saying, Glory to God in the highest, and on earth peace, good will toward men.

LUKE, 2:8-14

FROM THE REALMS OF GLORY *angels come to worship the Child. This is a detail from a Gozzoli fresco in Florence's Medici Palace.*

EXALTED
CHOIR
IN
SONGS OF PRAISE

PLAYING A LUTE, *an angel rejoices at Jesus' birth. The figure illuminates a decorative border in a medieval devotional book.*

NO FIGURES in the Christmas story are more delightful than the heavenly host of angels. Wise in their knowledge of God's ways, childlike in their direct speech and action, they burst upon the momentous events with a joy and a consideration for man that at once brings God closer to the simplest shepherds and emphasizes His awesome power and majesty. Glorifying God in heaven and offering peace and good will to men, the angels bring a touch of the divine to all who hear their message.

Angels appear suddenly and they act purposefully. For angels have a special role in the Bible that requires them to leave their place in God's firmament and to associate with His people on earth. Throughout the Old and New Testaments, the angels appear to man as messengers of God.

They bring comfort, as in Genesis when an angel advises the Egyptian maid Hagar that, if she returns to Abram and Sarai, her seed will multiply so that "it shall not be numbered for multitude."

Angels bring warnings, as when they announce to Lot the imminent destruction of Sodom and tell him to flee with his wife and daughters.

They bring tests of belief, as when Satan inflicts disease and death upon Job in a trial of his faith in God.

And they bring deliverance, too, as when Daniel says after a night in the lions' den that it was an angel who "hath shut the lions' mouths, that they have not hurt me."

Angels deliver perhaps the two most important messages in the life of Jesus. It is Gabriel who tells Mary that she shall bring forth a son of whose kingdom "there shall be no end." And it is also an angel, whose "countenance was like lightning," who rolls back the stone at the sepulcher and gives those who have come to mourn Jesus the message: "He is not here: for He is risen."

From these and other references, theologians have worked out an elaborate—but not always consistent—structure of the hierarchy and duties of the angels. They are ranked in this descending order of sublimity: seraphim, cherubim, thrones, dominions, virtues, powers, principalities, archangels and angels. Only archangels and angels, the two lowest orders, appear to man. Of these, the only ones to become known by name to man are the four archangels who, Hebrew tradition says, sustain the throne of god.

They are: Michael, captain general of the hosts of heaven in eternal combat with the Prince of Hell, who will sound his trumpet to awaken the dead for the Last Judgment; Gabriel, bearer of good news, who not only announced the coming of Jesus to Mary, but also told Daniel of the return of the Jews from captivity, and Zacharias that his wife Elizabeth would bear a son who would become John the Baptist; Raphael, chief of the guardian angels, who, tradition holds, brought the tidings of Christ's birth to the shepherds; and Uriel, who, as Christ's ambassador, appeared to the Apostles at Emmaus after His death. The duties of the others appear to be in heaven, guarding the throne of God, praising Him, doing His bidding and guarding men on earth.

The role of the guardian angels is illustrated by Jesus in Matthew 18:10 when He says of children: "Take heed that ye despise not one of these little ones; for I say unto you, that in heaven their angels do always behold the face of my Father...."

Angels have been favorites of such poets as Milton and of painters, though at first the Church forbade their representation. In the early Renaissance, artists usually depicted angels as severe-looking men with wings. Gradually, their features softened and they became boys with curling hair. Later, as in the Piero della Francesca at the right and the Fra Angelico *(following pages)*, they became quite feminine in appearance.

Angels have long been associated with music; to medieval scholastics and artists it seemed only natural that the angelic host should, by singing and playing, imitate the perfect harmony of heaven. And through the ages composers have set the angels' words to music.

Belief in angels is a matter of individual faith among Protestants. It is an article of faith in Roman Catholicism. Angels generally are described as having been created by God on a level that places them above man but beneath God himself. Satan was an angel of God until he fell. With him fell other angels, who became demons. Theologians disagree on whether they fell because of pride or because of jealousy of mankind. The question also arises whether Satan does the bidding of God, as when he gets the Lord's permission to tempt Job, or whether he is a being independent from and opposed to God.

STRUMMING RENAISSANCE LUTES, *angels sing at the Nativity in this late 15th Century work by Piero della Francesca. In this detail, Piero tried to suppress otherworldly elements; he omitted the angels' wings and halos. As heavenly beings, supernatural in freedom of spirit and ability to appear and disappear instantly on God's errands, angels are usually shown winged.*

THREE ANGEL MUSICIANS, *from a grouping of 12 by Fra Angelico, use medieval instruments to praise the Virgin and Child.*

AN ANGELIC
ENSEMBLE
IN
PRAISE TO GOD

In modern folklore, angels seem to play the harp almost to the exclusion of other musical instruments. But medieval painters and sculptors heard the music of the heavenly heralds in a different way. When de-picting angels, the artists furnished them with instruments of the artists' own time. In the examples on these and the following pages, the angel musicians are playing instruments well known in the 15th Century, yet not unlike many still in use today.

When he painted his triptych for the Linen Guild of Florence, Fra Angelico included an arch of 12 angels surrounding the Madonna and Child and praising them with an ensem-

ble that presages many modern musical instruments. Three of the celestial members of Fra Angelico's
grouping are shown above. The instruments they play are, from the
left: a *vièle,* an ancestor of all mod-

ern bowed string instruments; a
psaltery, an early relative of the
zither and of many other plucked
instruments; and a tambourine,
unchanged today and still familiar in orchestral percussion sections.

REJOICING ANGELS *attend Mary in a sec-
tion of a carved wood altarpiece representing
incidents from the Virgin's life (next pages).
Carved by the Master Arnt between 1483
and 1492, it is installed in the Church
of St. Nicholas in Calcar, Germany. The
angels are playing medieval instruments.*

WHY
ANGELS
HAVE
WINGS

Since the Bible gives few precise physical descriptions of angels, their appearance has been individually interpreted by artists and writers. The modern Christian, however, has a definite picture of angels fixed in his mind. How this image developed is traced by classicist Gilbert Highet in his article "An Iconography of Heavenly Beings," which is excerpted below.

HOW
IS IT, THEN,
THAT

whenever we hear the word "angel," we see a being with large wings? How is it that the image in our minds is a graceful shape with flowing robes and floating hair and kindly gaze, sexless or almost sexless, or perhaps with a hint of the feminine? God's messenger Gabriel, who spoke so authoritatively to Zacharias and Mary, was evidently masculine in form and nature. But painters have often depicted the angel of the Annunciation as a gentle visitor, like a maid of honor sent to pay homage to a princess; and the angel does not "come in" to Mary's room but flies down from heaven on a pair of birdlike wings.

This is because Christian art is a blend of Jewish mysticism and Greek imagery. The Jews, for whom the Old Testament and much of the New Testament were written, thought of God as being free of all bodily form and his messengers as human in appearance—mediums or diplomats, as it were, characterless save for their mission. But the Greeks, or at least the Greek artists and poets, could not think of the divine as formless, with no resemblance to humanity. To them, a god wore the shape of a perfect man or woman, endowed with superhuman powers. And the messenger of divinity must surely have the appurtenances of swift and graceful flight. Therefore Christian artists,

working in the Graeco-Roman tradition, gave their angels the wings of Victory and Eros and the Genius. But this did not happen all at once. Before the change was made, there was a long period of doubt and resistance. When the change did come, it was part of the great conversion of the pagan world.

THE
EARLIEST
CHRISTIAN

artists portray Jesus neither as an individual with distinctive features nor as a rabbi. Instead, they show him as one of the symbolic figures established by the vivid Greek imagination: Orpheus, teacher and poet, Hermes the friendly deity, carrying a lamb on his shoulders. In the same way, during the first four Christian centuries, angels are not shown as having wings. They are (as in the Scriptures) handsome youths, beardless, wearing ordinary clothes (ankle-length gown and cloak), standing or moving humanly upon the ground. But this was scarcely satisfactory. Artists wanted to distinguish the heavenly messengers from other young male figures such as the disciples of Jesus and Jesus himself. Greek and Roman Christian poets, elaborating on the Gospel stories, introduced traditional classical imagery. Thus, the good Paulinus of Nola, after describing the angel Gabriel's visit to Zacharias, concludes with something which is not in the Scriptures: "He spoke, and glided on wings into thin air." Mystics and divines reflected on the strange powers given by the Almighty to his envoys—their sudden appearances and disappearances, their rapid movement, their ubiquity—and concluded that, although human in form, they must be superhuman both in their beauty and in their power of flight.

ABOUT
A. D.
400,

after long suspense and mounting pressure, an ancient and enormous dam broke. The waters of the Christian spirit gushed into dry pagan channels, filling them with new energy and reviving much of the moribund life along their banks. Again and again, then and thereafter, we see pagan philosophical ideas, aesthetic patterns, imaginative symbols, and social and religious customs taken over by Christianity, rededicated and, without destruction, transformed. One of the oldest houses of worship in existence is the cathedral of Syracuse. It is simply the temple of Athena, built five centuries before Christ, and after twelve hundred years of paganism, converted into a Christian church. In the same way, the angels of Jewish and Christian Scripture took on the wings, the grace, and the spiritual intensity of Graeco-Roman spirits and demigods.

In Greek and Roman belief, an unseen guardian accompanies each of us from birth to death and (as Menander says) "initiates us into the mystic rites of life." He is our daemon, or our Genius. On sculptured tombs, the Genius sometimes appears at the moment of death, extinguishing his torch or, as the soul, flying away from the funeral pyre into heaven. This kindly companion gave his wings and something of his personality to the Christian angels.

THE IMAGE
OF
VICTORY

VICTORY had always accompanied the Roman emperors. When they, too, became Christians, she did not leave them. In the imperial palace at Constantinople the emperor's throne was flanked by two Victories with outspread wings, each holding a laurel crown. In Christian churches, too, the winged Victories now appeared, carrying the palms of triumph—as they did for Greek athletes at the great games, as the Jews did when they greeted Christ at his entry into Jerusalem, and as the blessed do standing before the throne of God in the Revelation of Saint John. In one strange, mystical picture from northern Italy, we see a procession centering on a winged female figure who stands beside a basket of bread and a cup of wine. The spirit is Victory, the bread and wine symbolize Jesus; and the two together mean *Christos Nika*, "Christ is Victorious!"

So it is that just as Greek and Roman temples became Christian houses of worship, just as subtle Greek philosophical thought and strong Roman organizing power were transfused into the Church, just as the wealth and vigor of Greek rhetoric and Roman poetry were put to the service of the new religion, so the messengers, the guardians, and the heavenly visitors of Graeco-Roman paganism gave their flight, their dignity, and their charm to the angels of Christian art and literature.

A PAPAL INTERPRETATION

Pope Pius XII (1876-1958) chose as his papal name the very quality for which he was most venerated by Roman Catholics. Once, addressing pilgrims from America, he again revealed his piety in these words about the guardian angels.

No one is so humble, but he has angels to attend him. So glorious, so pure, so wonderful they are, and yet they are given to be your fellow-wayfarers, charged to watch carefully over you, lest you fall away from Christ, their Lord. Not only they wish to defend you against dangers lurking along the way; they are also active at your side with a word of encouragement to your souls, as you strive to ascend higher and higher to closeness to God through Christ.

CHRISTMAS EVE

Angel voices mingle with Christmas bells in this thoughtful work by Robert Bridges (1844-1930), England's Poet Laureate for 17 years.

A Frosty Christmas-eve ' when the stars were shining
Fared I forth alone ' where westward falls the hill
And from many a village ' in the water'd valley
Distant music reached me ' peals of bells a-ringing:
The constellated sounds ' ran sprinkling on earth's floor
As the dark vault above ' with stars was spangled o'er.

Then sped my thought to keep ' that first Christmas of all
When the shepherds watching ' by their folds ere the dawn
Heard music in the fields ' and marvelling could not tell
Whether it were angels ' or the bright stars singing.

Now blessed be the towers ' that crown England so fair
That stand up strong in prayer ' unto God for our souls:
Blessed be their founders ' (said I) and our country-folk
Who are ringing for Christ ' in the belfries tonight
With arms lifted to clutch ' the rattling ropes that race
Into the dark above ' and the mad romping din.

But to me heard afar ' it was heav'nly music
Angels' song comforting ' as the comfort of Christ
When he spake tenderly ' to his sorrowful flock:
The old words came to me ' by the riches of time
Mellow'd and transfigured ' as I stood on the hill
Hark'ning in the aspect ' of th' eternal silence.

CARE IN HEAVEN?

It was a belief of the Renaissance that angels played a vigorous role in the affairs of man. It was in this context that Edmund Spenser (1552-1599) wrote, in his great epic "The Faerie Queene," these two stanzas in praise of angels.

And is there care in heaven? and is there love
In heavenly spirits to these creatures bace,
That may compassion of their evilles move?
There is: else much more wretched were the cace
Of men then beasts. But O! th' exceeding grace
Of highest God that loves his creatures so,
And all his workes with mercy doth embrace,
That blessed Angels he sends to and fro,
To serve to wicked man, to serve his wicked foe.

How oft do they their silver bowers leave,
To come to succour us that succour want!
How oft do they with golden pineons cleave
The flitting skyes, like flying Pursuivant,
Against fowle feendes to ayd us millitant!
They for us fight, they watch and dewly ward,
And their bright Squadrons round about us plant;
And all for love, and nothing for reward.
O! why should hevenly God to men have such regard?

A CLOUD OF ANGELS

The distinguished American Quaker leader Rufus M. Jones (1863-1948) once journeyed to Bethlehem for Christmas. His mystical experience there, which he describes in the extract from "The Shepherd Who Missed the Manger," attests to the Holy Land's ageless inspiration.

We sat under rustling olive trees and watched the sun sink over the Plains of Sharon and seem to fall into the Mediterranean beyond. Before sunset we had noticed strange masses of thin fleecy clouds, covering the sky, with areas of blue separating the clouds. But we thought nothing of it—they were just clouds, such as we have in America. But all of a sudden as the sun went out of sight these fleecy clouds began to turn red. In a little while the entire sky from the Mount of Olives in the East to the Great Sea in the West was filled with what looked like Seraphim, with outspread wings; for as everybody knows, I hope, the Seraphim, which are the highest order of angelic beings, are red—burning with love. And in between the red Seraphim were blue spaces which it was easy to imagine were Cherubim, for, as everybody knows, I am sure, Cherubim are always blue, and are the supreme knowers, "the great Intelligences," beholding the truth with their minds. Here just above our heads, on the Shepherds' Field, on Christmas Eve, was a sky full of what looked to us like Seraphim and Cherubim. We beheld it with awe and wonder, and though we heard no words from above, we said in our hearts "Glory to God in the highest." And under the spell of what we had seen, we silently climbed the hill to hear the midnight Christmas Service in the Church of the Nativity. Perhaps not twice in a thousand years would there come a sky like that—and we were there the night it came! I have forgotten the service that followed, but the memory of the sky full of Seraphim and Cherubim over the Shepherds' Field has never quite faded out of mind.

Within the Frame

In the popular imagination, angels changed slowly from grand figures to sentimentalized children. Kenneth Grahame (1859-1931), the author of the beloved children's story "The Wind in the Willows," was a boy when he and his brothers and sisters saw their first picture of classical angels. Grahame describes the episode in this excerpt from "Dream Days."

This left two or three more angels, who peeped or perched behind the main figures with a certain subdued drollery in their faces, as if the thing had gone on long enough, and it was now time to upset something or kick up a row of some sort. We knew these good folk to be saints and angels, because we had been told they were; otherwise we should never have guessed it. Angels, as we knew them in our Sunday books, were vapid, colourless, uninteresting characters, with straight up-and-down sort of figures, white nightgowns, white wings, and the same straight yellow hair parted in the middle. They were serious, even melancholy; and we had no desire to have any traffic with them. These bright bejewelled little persons, however, piquant of face and radiant of feather, were evidently hatched from quite a different egg, and we felt we might have interests in common with them. Short-nosed, shock-headed, with mouths that went up at the corners and with an evident disregard for all their fine clothes, they would be the best of good company, we felt sure, if only we could manage to get at them. One doubt alone disturbed my mind. In games requiring agility, those wings of theirs would give them a tremendous pull. Could they be trusted to play fair? I asked Selina, who replied scornfully that angels *always* played fair.

Angels We Have Heard on High

According to Luke, the angels said "Glory to God in the highest." Tradition insists they sang it, but angels' talk could well sound like song to man. In the French carol below, which celebrates the angelic message, their words appear in the chorus, which is sung in Latin.

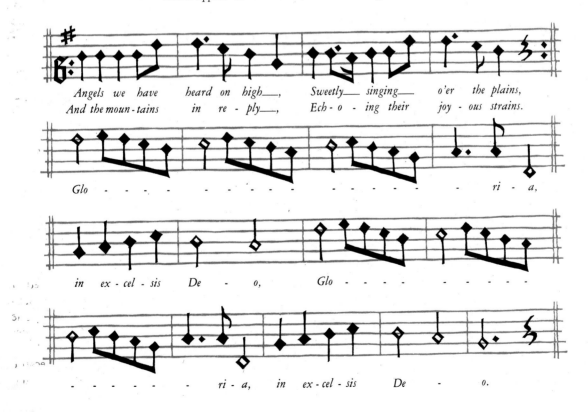

Angels we have heard on high___, Sweetly___ singing___ o'er the plains,
And the moun - tains in re - ply___, Ech - o - ing their joy - ous strains.

Glo - - - - - - - - - - - - - ri - a,

in ex - cel - sis De - o, Glo - - - - - - - -

- - - - - ri - a, in ex - cel - sis De - o.

V

THE FIRST WITNESSES

AND IT CAME TO PASS, AS THE angels were gone away from them into heaven, the shepherds said one to another, Let us now go even unto Bethlehem, and see this thing which is come to pass, which the Lord hath made known unto us. And they came with haste, and found Mary, and Joseph, and the babe lying in a manger. And when they had seen it, they made known abroad the saying which was told them concerning this child. And all they that heard it wondered at those things which were told them by the shepherds....And the shepherds returned, glorifying and praising God for all the things that they had heard and seen, as it was told unto them.

LUKE, 2:15-18, 20

GRIZZLED SHEPHERDS *receive the news of* *Jesus' birth from an angel in this painting* *by an unknown master of the 15th Century.*

LIFE
OF HARDSHIP
AND LOVE
OF THE FLOCK

IN A SHEPHERDS' FIELD, *a green-winged angel announces Jesus' birth. This vivid miniature was painted in the 15th Century.*

THE FIRST MEN to see and worship Jesus were shepherds. They were tending their sheep when the angel appeared in the night sky and told them the good news of His birth. "With haste" they led their flocks toward Bethlehem.

The winter rainy season had begun and the steep Judean hills streamed with rain. Nights were cold and there was often frost on the ground. When they could, the shepherds penned their flocks—goats intermingled with the sheep—in caves for the night, and when there were no caves they sheltered their sheep under trees and took refuge themselves in tents woven from goat hair. When they arrived in Bethlehem they could, they knew, pen their flocks in the natural caves in the hills outside the town.

They were rough and simple men —*am ha'aretz*, the common people —and they were armed against the dangers of their work. They carried weapons: a knife, a sling, a cudgel and a staff. Their clothes were those of the poor: a knee-length tunic, a sleeved jacket, and a coat made of sheepskin, tanned with the wool still on.

They were despised by the Sadducees for their poverty and dis-

trusted by the Pharisees for their careless observance of the law. Yet they were the first to worship the Child. They knelt and perhaps offered such gifts as they had: a cruse of oil, a piece of cheese, a fleece for a blanket.

They had little to give. Their life was frugal. They could take few stores on their long wanderings. At streams they caught fish and on the hills they snared birds. Fat from the sheep's tail, mixed with pellets of lean, was the only meat they carried with them. They carried a pouch of dough and made a crude bread by slapping the dough onto hot stones. They ate, if they were few, from one dish, scooping up food with wedges of bread. In spring and summer the ewes provided them with milk, butter and cheese. In spring, too, with the hard rains over and the pastures green, flocks fed easily again.

Spring was the start of the shepherd's year. In March and April the ewes, which had been bred five months before, lambed. The flock was shorn in May. Shearing was a festival time. After the sheep had been dipped in pools, and clipped, and then dipped again, the shepherds who had gathered at the pools celebrated with prayers, dances and songs. It was their harvesttime.

Then they moved northward into the hills until the hot winds dried up the hill fodder, forcing the flocks into the valleys below. Often, by autumn, the land was stripped bare. When the sheep had only thorns for food, the shepherd often brought them to carob trees, whose pods they ate, or to sycamores, whose fruit grew in clusters like figs.

Shepherds, in those days, led their sheep, they did not drive them. And each ram, ewe and lamb had a name.

When the shepherd called, the sheep came to his side. The shepherd led because, although he had dogs, his dogs did not muster the flock. They were guards. Shaggy and fierce, they fought off foxes, jackals and even wolves. Also, leading, the shepherd could guide his sheep away from grain fields where the flock would destroy the crop, or avoid fields in which weeds grew that could poison his sheep. With his staff he killed snakes in the way and with his sling he frightened off hawks.

To guide his flock, the shepherd needed to know the terrain in every detail—where the pasturage was good, where he could ford a river, where there were pure springs. And to keep the flock moving, he would have to carry a lamb if it were lame. "He shall feed his flock like a shepherd," Isaiah had said of the Messiah in his prophecy, "he shall gather the lambs with his arm, and carry them in his bosom, and shall gently lead those that are with young."

So it was fitting that the first witnesses of the birth of Jesus were shepherds, called up from their field where they sat by the fire.

In the pages which follow, these men of humble birth are shown in paintings, woodcuts and miniatures as medieval and earlier artists saw them. In each work these simple shepherds seem to know that their lowly station will be of no hindrance at Bethlehem, that they will be as welcome as the Kings who will come later. They appear to know that the Child whom they have been invited to see and to worship, the Child whom later generations would call "the good shepherd," would one day declare: "Whosoever therefore shall humble himself . . . the same is greatest in the kingdom of heaven."

WARMING THEIR HANDS, *two shepherds keep watch over their flock, penned for the night. An imaginary landscape of Bethlehem rises behind them. Sano di Pietro, the 15th Century Sienese artist who painted this scene, combined roughhewn realism with a deep sense of awe. The shepherds, sitting with their eyes upraised, seem ready to adore the Saviour they shall soon see.*

A PASTORAL SCENE *shows the musical instruments shepherds took with them to amuse themselves and calm their flocks. The shepherds in this French woodcut of 1497 have a bagpipe and, lying on the ground (right), two flutes. The Biblical herders also played pipes and small harps.*

A SOUND
OF MUSIC
IN THE FIELDS

For most of the year the shepherd's only company was his flock. During shearing time he might meet other herders at the dipping pool and with them celebrate the harvest of fleece, but otherwise he would avoid coming on land where others had been. He sought hills and valleys that were fresh, where the grass was uncropped.

Music helped the shepherd to pass his time, and he often led his flock while playing his flute. At evening, when he had sheltered the sheep, he played and sang.

So, artists of the Middle Ages, portraying the shepherds, gave them instruments to play on. And, since the artists saw history in terms of

their own times, they painted medieval forms of ancient instruments and dressed the Biblical herdsmen in medieval peasant clothes. In one Nativity play, a flute was the shepherds' first gift to Jesus. "There! Take it in thy hand! Wherein much pleasure have I found; and now . . . Thou shalt have it to make thee mirth."

A PIPING SHEPHERD *dances to his tune while a milkmaid milks and a dog bays at angels overhead. The landscape and the herder's life are romanticized in this 15th Century miniature.*

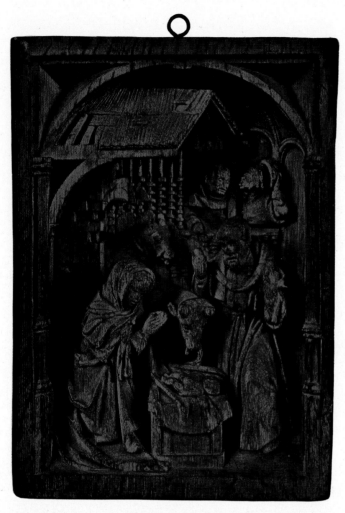

TWO HERDERS *peer into the manger in which Jesus lies. The setting and gestures are realistic in this Dutch wood carving of about 1500.*

THE SHEPHERDS
AT
THE MANGER

In Bethlehem the shepherds came to the stable, and in the stable they found Joseph, Mary and the Child, and they adored the Child. Jesus lay, according to an apocryphal tale, between an ox and an ass, and the animals too worshiped Him.

The scene inspired art and legend, for in the stable, God, man and the beasts of the earth were harmoniously and simply joined in gladness.

In many countries it became popular belief that on Christmas Eve, asses and oxen could speak and that then, as Shakespeare wrote, "the bird of dawning singeth all night long . . . the nights are wholesome, then no planets strike . . . so hallowed, and so gracious is the time." For the Nativity was the birth of hope; and the shepherds, having seen Jesus, left "glorifying and praising God."

AN ANGEL GUIDE *brings a shepherd to the place of Jesus' birth. The shepherd lifts his hand in wonder while, behind him, his companions watch the cloud of angels hovering overhead. Painted in the late 1400s by Crivelli, this masterpiece combines a formal style with an air of enchantment that seems to spread across the landscape and yet center in the shining Child.*

The Ox and the Ass

The Bible mentions no animals at Jesus' birth, but writers of apocryphal books often added the beasts. This example is from "Pseudo-Matthew."

Now on the third day after the nativity of our Lord Jesus Christ, the most blessed Mary went out of the cave, and, entering a stable, put her child in a manger, and the ox and ass adored him. Then was fulfilled that which was spoken by Isaiah the prophet, who said, The ox doth know his owner, and the ass his master's crib. The very animals, therefore, ox and ass, having him between them, incessantly adored him. Then was fulfilled that which was spoken by Habakkuk the prophet, who said, Between two animals thou art made known. In the same place Joseph tarried with Mary three days.

THE FRIENDLY BEASTS

This bit of Middle Ages' doggerel takes the assumption that animals were present at the nativity one step further: Its simple quatrains endow the animals with speech and generosity.

Jesus our Brother, kind and good,
Was humbly born in a stable rude,
And the friendly beasts around Him stood;
Jesus our Brother, kind and good.

"O," said the donkey, shaggy and brown,
"I carried His mother up hill and down;
I carried His mother to Bethlehem town."
"O," said the donkey, shaggy and brown.

"O," said the cow, all white and red,
"I gave Him my manger for His bed,
I gave Him my hay to pillow His head."
"O," said the cow, all white and red.

"O," said the sheep, with curly horn,
"I gave Him my wool for His blanket warm,
He wore my coat on Christmas morn."
"O," said the sheep, with curly horn.

Thus ev'ry beast by some good spell,
In the stable dark was glad to tell
Of the gift he gave Emmanuel,
The gift he gave Emmanuel.

The Gifts

With no scriptural justification, shepherds are often depicted as presenting gifts to Christ. But what would these poor and humble men have to give? The dialogue below, which comes from a 1480 calendar, "Le Grant Kalendrier des Bergiers," imagines the rough shepherds debating which of their meager possessions to proffer.

Aloris: Shepherds, we must think of everything. I am well advised we have not yet decided what gifts, and in what fashion, we will give to this Infant, when we see Him there.

Ysambert: Aloris, that is well said. We must think of it now.

Pellion: For myself, I have well decided what present I shall give, and a worthy one.

Rifflart: What, I pray you?

Pellion: Guess, and you will hear a good answer.

Rifflart: Will you give your crook? Or your fine rosary?

Pellion: You have not guessed. My crook is too necessary, I can do nothing without it; I doubt if He will get that.

Rifflart: Will you give Him your dog?

Pellion: Nenny, who would turn my sheep home for me?

Rifflart: Then you will give Him your stale bread, and a great heap of chestnuts?

Pellion: Nenny.

Rifflart: What will you give, then?

Pellion: I will give Him my flageolet, my new one; He cannot refuse it; it was never in Betlem before except when a little packman carried it: it cost me two good deniers . . .

Ysambert: I have thought of another gift—I will give Him a rattle marvellously well made, which goes *clic, clic,* at His ear, at least when the Infant cries this rattle will dry His tears, and He will be pacified.

Aloris: I will give Him something different—I have a fine kalendar in wood which tells the days and months, Lent and the new year: by it I can tell all feasts, I have never found a truer; every saint in it has his own picture. That will be an advantage to Him; at least when He is old enough, He may learn to read it.

Rifflart: It is a gift worth having, and worthy of being given to a Count; but for my part I am determined to give Him this little bell which hangs in my hat ever since the time of Robin Fouet; and with this, a very fine whirligig which I have in my bag.

The Carol of the Bagpipers

Every year just before Christmas, shepherd "zampognari" (bagpipers) from the mountains of Italy wander through the streets of Naples playing carols at roadside shrines.

While shep-herds watch did keep, O'er all their drows-ing sheep, From heav'n a voice came sing - - ing___: "Peace, Good-will be - fall." Come and a- dore___ him, Kneel down be-fore___Him: Seek___the Babe___ in yon-der stall. Your King tho weak___and small, For He this night a last - - -ing___ Light now shines for all.

69

VI
THE STORY OF THE MAGI

NOW WHEN JESUS WAS BORN IN Bethlehem of Judaea in the days of Herod the king, behold, there came wise men from the east to Jerusalem, Saying, Where is he that is born King of the Jews? for we have seen his star in the east, and are come to worship him. ...Then Herod, when he had privily called the wise men, inquired of them diligently what time the star appeared. And he sent them to Bethlehem and said, Go and search diligently for the young child; and when ye have found him, bring me word again, that I may come and worship him also. When they had heard the king, they departed; and, lo, the star, which they saw in the east, went before them, till it came and stood over where the young child was. When they saw the star, they rejoiced with exceeding great joy. And when they were come into the house, they saw the young child with Mary his mother, and fell down, and worshipped him: and when they had opened their treasures, they presented unto him gifts; gold, and frankincense, and myrrh.

MATTHEW, 2:1-2, 7-11

RICHLY ROBED *in the garb of a Floren-*
tine noble, a Wise Man is shown riding to
the manger in this 15th Century work.

ROYAL
JOURNEY
TO
BETHLEHEM

THE RENDEZVOUS *of the Kings at a cross-roads outside Paris is fancifully shown in the famous Duc de Berry Book of Hours.*

WHEN it became known that the Son of God was born to Mary, both rich and poor bowed in worship to Him. At one end of the scale were the shepherds mentioned in Luke, humbly adoring in the manner of simple folk everywhere. At the other end were the figures Matthew calls Wise Men (called in other sources Magi), whose reverence has come to symbolize the submission of worldly power to Christ's divine authority. The brief account in Matthew (condensed on the previous page) is the only mention of these Wise Men in the Bible. It does not name them, say where they came from or even how many there were.

Gradually, over a long period of years after Matthew's account was written, a remarkable thing occurred: the Wise Men began to take on individuality. Each acquired a name, a background, a life story. Still subsidiary in the Christmas drama, they took on leading roles in a legend of their own. They were venerated on a Church holiday—Epiphany—January 6, at first commemorated as the anniversary of the baptism of Christ but later celebrated in many lands as Three Kings Day as well. Well past the Renaissance the grip of the Magi on the popular mind kept growing, for one reason: people wanted to believe the story.

The appeal of the Magi is magical. To them alone, the Bible states, appeared the star miraculously heralding Christ's birth. Responding as to a command, they set forth with exotic gifts. The star guided them surely, while Herod the king had to ask them to bring him word of where Jesus lay. And when divine intervention kept them from revealing His location, Christ's life was saved, for Herod had professed a desire to worship the newcomer but actually meant to slay Him.

On this scriptural framework the legend was embroidered by churchmen and by lay students, authors, artists, composers. One step was to transform "wise men" into "kings." The original word "Magi" in the Latin version of the Scriptures refers to Persian priest-astrologers; later embellishments added the meaning of men of wisdom—doctors or philosophers. But in the Second Century the scholar Tertullian linked the Magi with two Old Testament prophecies that kings bearing gifts would come to Israel. By the end of the Sixth Century, "kings" and "Magi" were used interchangeably.

At about the same time the Magi became Kings, their number was being settled. Early Church art shows either two or four. St. Augustine favored 12, for its symbolic connotation of the number of the tribes of Israel and Christ's Apostles. Then papal choice in the Second Century settled on three because Matthew mentions three gifts.

By the Eighth Century the Kings had names and physical attributes. Melchior was seen as an old man, Balthazar as mature and Gaspar as a young man. Each was given a domain. Balthazar, for example, was identified with Ethiopia and frequently depicted as a Negro.

These and many other details were collected about 1370 in *The Story of the Three Kings* by a monk, John of Hildesheim. A comparable account appears in *The Golden Legend,* an earlier work by Jacobus de Voragine. Both narratives, while differing in particulars, agree on the broad outline of the legends.

In John's account the Magi met on their journey to the manger near the hill of Calvary and, despite their diverse origins, spoke freely with each other in a common tongue. Together they traveled on until they came to "the little house where Christ was. . . ." John says, "He was somewhat fat."

Contemporary paintings may well have inspired such descriptions. As the legend spread, artists undertook to visualize its meaningful moments with brush or chisel. Each came to his subject differently, and sometimes the result was more elegant than pious. Most, however, were moved by the spirit of the Magi legend: the reverent adoration of the Christ child by the three Wise Men.

THE THREE KINGS AND HEROD *are dramatically portrayed in this sculpture in the cathedral at Ulm, Germany. Herod, at right, admonished the Kings to return and tell him where they found Jesus, so that he too might go and worship Him. The Kings (crowned figures at center), unaware that Herod planned to kill Jesus, agreed to his demand. But later an angel told them of the danger.*

ORNATE CONTAINERS *for the gifts of the Magi are singled out from a Dutch painting of the 1500s. Above: round box for the gold.*

VESSEL FOR FRANKINCENSE *probably duplicates an actual metal piece, perhaps a ceremonial container for church or court use.*

URN FOR MYRRH *is in Balthazar's hand. Melchior usually is first in line, giving the gold, Gaspar to one side with frankincense.*

THE REGAL GIFTS OF THE MAGI

The presentation of their gifts to Jesus and their adoration of Him—at once the aim and the climax of the Kings' journey—have moved men's minds for centuries. Kneeling in tribute *(opposite)*, the Magi express the love and awe Christ evokes in all who believe in Him.

What gifts were judged suitable to such a moment? The Bible names them: gold, frankincense and myrrh. Each has its obvious worth. Gold is a valuable metal; frankincense and myrrh are aromatic resins from the bark of African trees *(right)*, valued for incense. Beyond these practical purposes are rich symbolic meanings.

Many church scholars consider the gold to mean love or Christ as King of the world; the frankincense (a very sweet spice), prayer or Christ as King of Heaven; the myrrh (from a thorny tree), suffering or a symbol of Christ's approaching sacrifice. Jacobus de Voragine suggests pragmatically that the gold was intended to ease Mary's poverty, the frankincense to ward off stable smells and the myrrh to deter the stable's vermin.

FRANKINCENSE   MYRRH

Since the Bible does not mention containers for the gifts, artists created them. A small casket often is shown for gold coins, a vessel for frankincense, an urn for myrrh.

At some point in the development of the Magi legend, its central figures passed into folklore and were made responsible for distributing gifts to good children on Three Kings Day. In most lands this Christmas function ultimately fell to Santa Claus, St. Nicholas or some other personage, but the Kings still delight children in most of Spain and Spanish America. Their first gifts to Jesus—love and devotion—set a pattern now almost universal on Christ's birthday.

KNEELING KINGS *appear in a detail of a mosaic by Pietro Cavallini (about 1290) in Rome's Santa Maria Church in Trastevere.*

"ADORATION OF THE MAGI" *was done in oil by Sandro Botticelli about 1480 (**next** pages). Before a classical structure in an Italian landscape surrounded by shepherds **and** attendants in contemporary Florentine dress, the Three Kings offer their traditional gifts to the infant Jesus. Though the artist was tempted to produce a scene of fashionable pageantry, a quietly reverent mood prevails. Besides paintings by Renaissance masters, the Adoration of the Magi has been rendered in graphic media from stained glass to whalebone by artists all over the world.*

AFTER BETHLEHEM

According to Matthew, the Wise Men were "warned in a dream" not to go back to Herod after seeing Jesus in Bethlehem, so "they departed into their own country another way." The stylized 12th Century stone carving above, credited to Gislebertus and found in the Cathedral of St.-Lazare in Autun, France, shows the Kings, three in a bed and serene of mind as an angel awakens them with God's warning. This sleep scene later came

to be considered undignified and was not depicted after the 16th Century.

The Bible is silent on the Kings after their departure for home. Not so John of Hildesheim, whose imaginative account (excerpted on the following pages) includes their death and burial in one tomb. Historically, three bodies said to be the Kings were taken from Milan to Cologne in 1164. A handsome shrine was erected and the "Three Kings of Cologne" attracted visitors from all Europe. Both the shrine and the bodies now are vanished, and with them much belief in this legend of the Magi. Still the tradition lives on and continues to enrich the Christmas story.

What Befell the Kings Later

John of Hildesheim, already cited in this chapter, made the definitive collection of the legends that had been accumulating for centuries about the Three Kings. This work was done at some point between 1364, when the Bishop of Münster asked the Carmelite monk to undertake it, and 1373, the year John died. "The Story of the Three Kings" was written in Latin, later translated into other languages. The English version from which the excerpt below was taken is an adaptation by Margaret Freeman. It takes the Kings from India (where astrologers allegedly had watched from the Hill of Vaus for a star that would herald the Messiah) along their several roads to Jerusalem. It has them meeting the shepherds and presenting gifts to them before going on to the stable where Jesus lay and offering Him gold, frankincense and myrrh. Then the book follows them home again and, in the chapters below, tells how they founded a city called Suwella, chose Prester John to rule there, then died—all probably imaginary, but described with faith and love. The illustrations used here are from woodcuts in an edition of "The Three Kings" printed in Strasbourg in 1484.

Then these three Kings with all their people went with Saint Thomas the Apostle to the Hill of Vaus; and there Saint Thomas hallowed the chapel that the three Kings had built there. And Saint Thomas and these three Kings preached to the people in that chapel concerning the Christian faith and the star that had appeared to the three Kings.

And the fame of these three Kings and of Saint Thomas spread to all the lands about and so great was their renown that all manner of men and women came from divers countries to visit the chapel on the Hill of Vaus. And from the great concourse of people that came to this chapel, the three Kings ordained a fair city and a rich one, which is called Suwella.

God is evermore wonderful in his work, for when Saint Thomas had thus preached and converted the people to the Christian belief, then he ordained and consecrated these three Kings as archbishops. And they then ordained other bishops, priests and clerks to serve God. Also Saint Thomas taught them all the manner and form of saying mass; also he taught them the words that Christ had said at supper the night that he was betrayed, and the Paternoster and many other things. He told them also the form of baptising and especially he charged them that they should never forget that. And when Saint Thomas had informed these three Kings and all the other people of the faith, then he went forth to other cities and towns and preached. And then he suffered martyrdom for the love of Christ.

And ye shall understand that in that country where Saint Thomas was slain, both men and women have visages like hounds.

After the death of Saint Thomas these three Kings who were archbishops did hallow all the temples in the country to the worship of Our Lady and cast out all the idols in the temples and ordained bishops and priests and clerks. And to these bishops, priests and clerks the three

Kings gave many possessions to maintain God's service.

Then these three Kings forsook the vanity of the world and abode in the city of Suwella, which they had founded, as it was aforesaid, and all the people about them did venerate them and love them.

And the second year before the death of these

three Kings they did call together all the kings and princes and bishops of their lands, for they were now in the last age of their lives and they had no children nor heirs; neither had they ever had queens or concubines as is the common usage of all the country. And this is found in all the writings and books of the East, though a German chronicler says the contrary of Melchior, who, according to these writings, had a wife and by her a child.

And when all the people were gathered together, the three Kings, with the assent of the people, chose a man among them who should be spiritual head in Saint Thomas' place and who should be called Patriarch Thomas. And the first patriarch that was thus chosen was a man called Jacob who had come with Saint Thomas from Antioch to India.

When the Patriarch Thomas was thus chosen, then these three Kings with the common assent of all the people chose and ordained a worshipful and mighty lord who should be temporal head and governor. And they ordained that this lord should not be called King or Emperor but Prester John, in veneration of Saint John the Evangelist and also Saint John the Baptist. And so the names of these lords continue yet unto this day.

And when this was done all the people went home again with great joy and these three Kings abode still in the city of Suwella.

N ow these three Kings lived together for two more years in the city of Suwella which they had founded near the Hill of Vaus. Then a little while before the feast of the Nativity of Our Lord Jesus Christ there appeared a wonderful star above the city, by which star the three Kings understood that the time was nigh when they should pass out of this world. Wherefore they did make a fair great tomb for their burial in the same church that they had there ordained. And in that same church these three Kings on the feast of Christmas did celebrate solemnly divine service.

Now on the eighth day after the birth of Christ, Melchior, who was King of Arabia and Nubia, said mass solemnly in the church, and at that time he was a hundred and sixteen years old. And when he had said mass he laid himself down, and without any disease, he yielded up to Our Lord God his spirit and so died. And the other two Kings came and took his body and arrayed it with bishops' ornaments and bore him to his tomb and there they laid him.

Then on the feast of the Epiphany, Balthasar, who was King of Saba, said devoutly his mass. And when mass was done, without any grievance he

passed out of this world to the bliss that is everlasting. And the years of his age were a hundred and twelve. So Jaspar, the third King, and other men took up this King, and when they had arrayed him as he should be, they laid him beside Melchior, his fellow, in the same tomb.

And then the sixth day after that, Jaspar, who was King of Tharsis, when he had offered the blessed sacrament on the altar and with all devotion had said his mass, then Christ took to him his spirit to dwell with him in everlasting joy. And so before all the people he died. And the years of his age were a

hundred and nine. Then the people came and took his body and arrayed it worshipfully and bore it to the same tomb where these other two Kings lay. And then this wonder Christ showed there before all the people: when the body of the third King was brought to be laid in the tomb beside the two Kings, anon each one of the two Kings moved apart from the other and gave room for Jaspar in the middle place.

And so as these three glorious Kings lived together in life, they were not parted in their death. And these three Kings in their tomb seemed to the people not as dead bodies but as men who were asleep. And they remained whole and incorrupt many years and days afterwards.

And the star that appeared over the city before their death abode there always still, until the bodies of the three Kings were moved away.

A long time after the death of these three Kings the Christian faith stood and was in prosperity in the worshipful city of Suwella and in all the Kingdoms of the East. Then the devil through his wicked angels excited among the people divers errors and opinions of heresy in the lands of the East, and also in Suwella where these three Kings rested. And the people turned again to their old law and worshipped false gods and forsook the law of God; so that these three Kings were held in no reverence and were almost forgotten. And whereas their bodies had remained incorrupt before, now they dissolved and turned into powder.

And those people dwelling at that time in Suwella who had come from the lands and kingdoms of these three Kings, each group took its King out of the tomb and put him into a separate chest and bore him home to his own land and kingdom. And there each King remained for a long time afterward, each in his own country.

JOURNEY OF THE MAGI

From the quaintness of John of Hildesheim to the realism of T. S. Eliot seems a far cry, but the modern poet shares John's interest in myth. In the work below he adds a disturbing philosophical consideration to the story of the Magi.

"A cold coming we had of it,
Just the worst time of the year
For a journey, and such a long journey:
The ways deep and the weather sharp,
The very dead of winter."
And the camels galled, sore-footed, refractory,
Lying down in the melting snow.
There were times we regretted
The summer palaces on slopes, the terraces,
And the silken girls bringing sherbet.
Then the camel men cursing and grumbling
And running away, and wanting their liquor and women,
And the night-fires going out, and the lack of shelters,
And the cities hostile and the towns unfriendly
And the villages dirty and charging high prices:
A hard time we had of it.
At the end we preferred to travel all night,
Sleeping in snatches,
With the voices singing in our ears, saying
That this was all folly.

Then at dawn we came down to a temperate valley,
Wet, below the snow line, smelling of vegetation;
With a running stream and a water-mill beating the darkness,
And three trees on the low sky,
And an old white horse galloped away in the meadow.
Then we came to a tavern with vine-leaves over the lintel,
Six hands at an open door dicing for pieces of silver,
And feet kicking the empty wine-skins.
But there was no information, and so we continued
And arrived at evening, not a moment too soon
Finding the place; it was (you may say) satisfactory.

All this was a long time ago, I remember,
And I would do it again, but set down
This set down
This: were we led all that way for
Birth or Death? There was a Birth, certainly,
We had evidence and no doubt. I had seen birth and death,
But had thought they were different; this Birth was
Hard and bitter agony for us, like Death, our death.
We returned to our places, these Kingdoms,
But no longer at ease here, in the old dispensation,
With an alien people clutching their gods.
I should be glad of another death.

This 19th Century work by Henry Wadsworth Longfellow is traditional in form and thought in its treatment of the theme of the Kings. The passage below is taken from a poem whose special appeal lies in its sensuous imagery.

Three Kings came riding from far away,
Melchior and Gaspar and Baltasar;
Three Wise Men out of the East were they,
And they travelled by night and they slept by day,
For their guide was a beautiful, wonderful star. . .
Three caskets they bore on their saddle-bows,
Three caskets of gold with golden keys;
Their robes were of crimson silk, with rows
Of bells and pomegranates and furbelows,
Their turbans like blossoming almond-trees. . .
They laid their offerings at his feet:
The gold was their tribute to a King;
The frankincense, with its odor sweet,
Was for the Priest, the Paraclete;
The myrrh for the body's burying.

Nicolas Roi Mage

The magic of the Three Kings' story has captured the imagination of all ages. This account of a fourth Wise Man is the work of the French author Roger Vercel (1894-1957), translated and adapted by Audrey Foote.

We were celebrating Epiphany at the home of my friend, Dr. Herve, and I had found the bean in my portion of the cake. I extricated the bean from the cake and held it up, careful to assume that particular expression, both smug and idiotic, which is considered proper form on such an occasion. The usual ritual followed: the choice of a queen and then toasts, punctuated with the traditional "The King Drinks!" The doctor had watched this playful ceremony with noticeable distraction. Suddenly he remarked,

"This reminds me that I once knew a Mage."

"Ah! Which of the three?" I asked.

"The fourth," Herve answered.

And then he told us the following story:

It was 12 years ago, and I had just arrived in Brittany. Like so many young men starting out, I had a little second-hand automobile. It was a sturdy enough little car but one fine night in December it stopped dead, right in the middle of the barren countryside.

A half hour passed during which I loosened a screw here, cleaned off a wire there; alternating with this routine, I tried spinning the crank. Nothing worked. Already night was falling and I began to wonder nervously if another turn of the crank might get it started or whether I would have to go through it all again in the pitch dark; I straightened up once more from under the hood to find standing beside me a bizarre figure, watching me.

He was a man of about 50 with a grey beard and long hair. He was thin as a lath. He was dressed in a shirt and trousers like those of a harlequin, made of various scraps of material but sewn together with care.

I admit that this encounter, in that solitude, was disquieting. The immobility, the silence of the man —appearing out of nowhere—were not reassuring. I did what one does in such cases: I pretended not to notice this strange spectator and I began again to crank the engine with redoubled energy and no success.

The bizarre figure beside me suddenly said, "There's something wrong with the ignition."

I had begun to suspect as much, but it greatly pleased me to hear *him* say it. Somehow the remark stripped him of mystery and clothed him in an air of reassuring normality.

He added, "I've played around some with motors; would you like me to look at it?"

He was welcome to try, I said. As I had done, he loosened a screw, cleaned a wire, but apparently in the right places. "Now it has some juice."

And, in fact, the engine started at the first try. I thanked my good samaritan with true gratitude. But his next remark jolted me back to my first feelings of disquiet:

"It's a good thing this didn't happen a half hour later for I wouldn't have been here to fix it; it's the hour when I enter the Throne Room."

This declaration rendered the countryside, already darkening, more hostile and menacing than ever. I repeated a hasty thanks, bounded into the seat and drove off with a sensation of deliverance.

Naturally I spoke to my acquaintances of my encounter.

"Ah," they said. "You have met Nicolas."

I learned that my mechanic was a former sailor who had literally fallen on his head; one day on a voyage to Newfoundland he had toppled head first from the mainmast where he was reefing a tops'l. Since then, he became a King every night as soon as he fell asleep.

Understand me: he was not crazy. But whereas *our* dreams are varied and unrelated, he took up the same dream each night and at the very point he had left it the night before. And in his dream, this simple peasant led the existence of an oriental King.

"He doesn't like summer," my friends said. "The nights are too short."

Thus acquainted with his case, I made certain I saw him often.

I do not believe that there could exist a happier being than that one, for whom daily life was but a negligible incident, and who saw open each night the doors of a magical domain. I even began to envy him a little, comparing his nights with my own; for I was often awakened by the frantic ring

83

of the doorbell and would have to set out, only half awake, to grope my way through the dirty little streets of the village.

Despite his regal, second life, Nicolas was troubled. One night in January I found him agitated to the point of frenzy. Things were not going well at the Palace. Certain envious persons were trying to overthrow him, to suborn his servants and his guards, to put themselves on his throne. But if they were looking for a fight, they'd find one! There would be a real brawl, even if it meant the end of him.

This fantasy revolution struck me as a very real menace; I realized immediately that Nicolas risked violent madness. I sought, without finding, the means to rescue him.

I had to leave him on the doorstep of his cottage, somber, tense, ready for sleep, but this time to confront the terrifying enemies which his dream would call forth. I went straight to the parsonage and I recounted the whole affair to the curé.

"If you have an idea, abbé—"

He *had* an idea, and it was a good one.

He went to find Nicolas and said to him:

"If I were in your place, do you know what I would do? I would depart immediately for Bethlehem. It will soon be Epiphany; this is the moment when the Kings begin their journey. I would gather around me all the loyal fellows I could find —there must be a few left?"

"Yes," Nicolas admitted. "I still have a few loyal buddies."

"Well then!" said the abbé. "I would lead them right off to Bethlehem. One couldn't lose one's way; one has only to follow the star. And once there, I'm sure I would be well received. And to come and bother me there with the baby Jesus? Just let them try! . . . There were only three kings so you will be the fourth and that will be all to the good: I have always thought that Brittany ought to have sent someone."

Nicolas left that very night for the crèche with his entourage. And as the abbé had predicted, he was well received, so well in fact that when I saw him again I found him radiant, his face all illuminated from within.

Once arrived at the crèche, he stayed there—for he died on Chandeleur. I never saw a sweeter death. His last words were:

"The Little One will be content."

And, without being in on the secrets of heaven, I believe the "Little One" was content.

Frankincense and Myrrh

Many writers have taken liberties in interpreting the gifts and the personalities of the three Wise Men. In the following story, the American newspaperman Heywood Broun (1888-1939) invents another present for Jesus—a gift that proves one of the Wise Men truly wise.

Once there were three kings in the East and they were wise men. They read the heavens and they saw a certain strange star by which they knew that in a distant land the King of the World was to be born. The star beckoned to them and they made preparations for a long journey.

From their palaces they gathered rich gifts, gold and frankincense and myrrh. Great sacks of precious stuffs were loaded on the backs of the camels which were to bear them on their journey. Everything was in readiness, but one of the wise men seemed perplexed and would not come at once to join his two companions, who were eager and impatient to be on their way in the direction indicated by the star.

They were old, these two kings, and the other wise man was young. When they asked him he could not tell why he waited. He knew that his treasures had been ransacked for rich gifts for the King of Kings. It seemed that there was nothing more which he could give, and yet he was not content.

He made no answer to the old men who shouted to him that the time had come. The camels were impatient and swayed and snarled. The shadows across the desert grew longer. And still the young king sat and thought deeply.

At length he smiled, and he ordered his servants to open the great treasure sack upon the back of the first of his camels. Then he went into a high chamber to which he had not been since he was a child. He rummaged about and presently came out and approached the caravan. In his hand he carried something which glinted in the sun.

The kings thought that he carried some new gift more rare and precious than any which they had been able to find in all their treasure rooms. They bent down to see, and even the camel drivers peered from the backs of the great beasts to find out what it was which gleamed in the sun. They were curious about this last gift for which all the caravan had waited.

And the young king took a toy from his hand and placed it upon the sand. It was a dog of tin, painted white, and speckled with black spots. Great patches of paint had worn away and left the metal clear, and that was why the toy shone in the sun as if it had been silver.

The youngest of the wise men turned a key in the side of the little black and white dog and then he stepped aside so that the kings and the camel drivers could see. The dog leaped high in the air and turned a somersault. He turned another and another and then fell over on his side and lay there with a set and painted grin upon his face.

A child, the son of a camel driver, laughed and clapped his hands, but the kings were stern. They rebuked the youngest of the wise men and he paid no attention but called to his chief servant to make the first of all the camels kneel. Then he picked up the toy of tin and, opening the treasure sack, placed his last gift with his own hands in the mouth of the sack so that it rested safely upon the soft bags of incense.

"What folly has seized you?" cried the eldest of the wise men. "Is this a gift to bear to the King of Kings in the far country?"

And the young man answered and said: "For the King of Kings there are gifts of great richness, gold and frankincense and myrrh.

"But this," he said, "is for the child in Bethlehem."

The Golden Carol of the Three Wise Men

One of the oldest English carols, hard to date but suggesting medieval music in its persistent rhythmic motion, is the "Golden Carol" sung on Twelfth Night. Many such carols originated as the music announcing the Three Kings in various medieval miracle and mystery plays.

We saw a light shine out a-far, On Christmas in the morn -ing.
And straight we knew it was Christ's star, Bright beam-ing in the morn -ing.

Then did we fall on bend-ed knee, On Christmas in the morn - ing,

And praised the Lord, who'd let us see His glo- ry at its dawn- ing.

VII

A LEGACY OF LOVE

IN THE BEGINNING WAS THE Word, and the Word was with God, and the Word was God. The same was in the beginning with God. All things were made by him; and without him was not any thing made that was made. In him was life; and the life was the light of men. And the light shineth in darkness; and the darkness comprehended it not. . . . He came unto his own, and his own received him not. But as many as received him, to them gave he power to become the sons of God, even to them that believe on his name: Which were born, not of blood, nor of the will of the flesh, nor of the will of man, but of God. And the Word was made flesh, and dwelt among us, (and we beheld his glory, the glory as of the only begotten of the Father,) full of grace and truth. JOHN, 1:1-5, 11-14

CHRIST'S ASCENSION *fulfills the promise of His birth. Seen opposite is Giotto's version, a 1305 fresco in the Arena Chapel at Padua.*

A LIFE,
A LESSON
FOR MANKIND

JESUS IN TRIUMPH *enters Jerusalem, as prophesied by Zechariah. The Latin echoes Zechariah, "In the eighth month. . . ."*

CHRISTMASTIDE ends with Epiphany. This is the manifestation of Christ to the Gentiles, in the persons of the Magi. Thus the close of Christmas opens the greater narrative of Christ's life, His ministry and His legacy to all mankind.

The Gospels tell us little about Jesus' early years. The Holy Family fled from Bethlehem into Egypt to escape the efforts of King Herod to destroy "the young child" who the wise men had told him was "born King of the Jews." After the death of Herod (when Jesus was two or three), the Holy Family went back to Joseph's hometown of Nazareth. There "the child grew, and waxed strong in spirit, filled with wisdom; and the grace of God was upon him."

Joseph was a carpenter. Medieval tradition had it that he died when Jesus was 19, and that the young man took over the business. Some scholars think He may have been influenced by the Essenes, the sect which composed and preserved the manuscripts now known as the Dead Sea Scrolls. No one knows. What *is* known is that

His time was an age of change. Both the Judaic and Roman cultures had fallen under the influence of Hellenism, and the Roman system was showing the first signs of the interior corruption that would later cause its military defeat. It was an apocalyptic time, ripe for the coming of the Messiah who would restore Israel as a great nation.

In those days came John the Baptist, preaching in the wilderness of Judea, And saying, Repent ye: for the kingdom of heaven is at hand." John, the son of Mary's cousin Elizabeth, was, in fulfillment of Isaiah's prophecy, the "voice of him that crieth in the wilderness, Prepare ye the way of the Lord." He baptized Jesus, and "lo, the heavens were opened unto him, and he saw the Spirit of God descending like a dove, and lighting upon him: And lo a voice from heaven, saying, This is my beloved Son, in whom I am well pleased."

Christ's ministry had begun. But He brought not the promise of a political kingdom for one nation, but the gospel of the kingdom of God, which is "within you."

Jesus' ministry took the form of deeds and words. The deeds, demonstrations of His boundless love, mercy and charity, are often miracles of healing—of the blind and dumb, of the palsied and lame, of lepers and madmen, and of the dead restored to life. They are demonstrations of the power of love and hope combined. "Thy faith hath made thee whole," said Christ.

The words of Christ's ministry are outwardly simple, concerned with homely subjects—bread and wine, fishing and farming—but they carry a revolutionary message. Jesus stated: "Verily, verily, I say unto thee, Except a man be born again, he

cannot see the kingdom of God."

His teaching was grounded solidly in the Old Testament. "Thou shalt love the Lord thy God with all thy heart, and with all thy soul, and with all thy mind. This is the first and great commandment. And the second is like unto it, Thou shalt love thy neighbor as thyself. On these two commandments hang all the law and the prophets."

"Think not that I am come to destroy the law, or the prophets," He declared in the Sermon on the Mount, "I am not come to destroy, but to fulfill." In fulfilling, he refined and transformed the old precepts: "It hath been said, Thou shalt love thy neighbor, and hate thine enemy. But I say unto you, Love your enemies, bless them that curse you, do good to them that hate you, and pray for them which despitefully use you, and persecute you."

This is a demanding doctrine but one which excludes no one: "I say unto you that . . . joy shall be in heaven over one sinner that repenteth, more than over ninety and nine just persons, which need no repentance."

For those who would not obey the commands of His teaching, Christ foresaw "outer darkness . . . weeping and gnashing of teeth." But to the humble, the merciful—to all erring human beings who truly repent —He made the promise: "Ask, and it shall be given you; seek, and ye shall find; knock, and it shall be opened unto you."

Christ's words (John 15:11) sum up the essence of Christianity. "These things have I spoken unto you, that my joy might remain in you, and that your joy might be full. This is my commandment, That ye love one another as I have loved you."

That is Christ's legacy to mankind.

"THE HEAD OF CHRIST," *by Georges Rouault, shows a compassionate Jesus who might be saying, "Suffer the little children to come unto me and forbid them not: for of such is the Kingdom of God." One of a large number of heads of Jesus painted by Rouault in the late 1930s, this one is owned by the Cleveland Museum of Art. Many in the same series show Christ being mocked.*

MIRACLES
AND MYSTERIES

At the heart of Christianity is faith in the miracle of God's incarnation in the Son of Man and of the Son of Man's triumph over death. The theme has inspired countless paintings, many as radiantly mystical as these three panels from the great altarpiece painted about 1515 by the German master Grünewald. The altarpiece is now displayed in the Unterlinden Museen in Colmar, France.

In the panel at the left, Grünewald portrays the Annunciation. As the angel Gabriel appears, and the dove

of the Holy Spirit hovers in the background of the little chapel, Mary's Bible opens to the prophecy of Isaiah: "Behold, a virgin shall conceive, and bear a son. . . ." Above her, a sculptured figure of Isaiah waits for the fulfillment of his prophecy.

The central panel depicts two Nativity scenes. Within the shrine (rear), Mary, surrounded by angelic musicians, awaits the birth of the Child. In the foreground, she holds the newborn Christ, while the celestial host proclaims the tidings of great joy.

In the panel at the right, the Resurrection marks the ultimate triumph of the spirit. Christ, enveloped in a divine radiance, rises from the tomb into the starry firmament, a token to all who will receive Him of hope and deliverance for all of mankind.

CHRIST'S LIFE, A GIFT TO THE WORLD

Throughout the Middle Ages the art that adorned every church helped to familiarize the people with the details of the Gospel stories as well as to keep a constant reminder before the faithful. This remarkable example is a pictorial biography of Christ —not unlike a comic strip in form. Now in the Berlin-Dahlem Staatliche Museen, it was painted about 1400 by a German artist known only as the Cologne Master. Thirty-four of the panels pertain to Christ, the 35th shows the work's donors. From left to right, the scenes are:

Top row: 1) The Annunciation; 2) The Visitation; 3) Mary and Joseph Going to Bethlehem; 4) The Manger; 5) The Circumcision; 6) The Adoration of the Magi; 7) The Presentation in the Temple.

Second row: 1) Christ in the Temple at 12; 2) His Childhood *(top)* and Baptism *(bottom);* 3) Christ Preaching; 4) The Entry into Jerusalem; 5) The Last Supper; 6) Christ Washing the Disciples' Feet; 7) The Agony in the Garden.

Third row: 1) The Awakening of the Apostles; 2) The Kiss of Judas; 3) Christ before Herod; 4) Christ before the High Priest; 5) Christ before Pilate; 6) The Scourging; 7) The Crown of Thorns.

Fourth row: 1) Pilate Washes His Hands; 2) Christ Carrying the Cross; 3) Christ Is Disrobed; 4) Christ Is Nailed to the Cross; 5) The Crucifixion; 6) The Descent from the Cross; 7) The *Pietà,* or Mourning of the Virgin over Christ's Body.

Fifth row: 1) The Lamentation; 2) The Resurrection *(bottom)* and The Descent into Hell; 3) The Ascension of Christ; 4) The Descent of the Holy Ghost; 5) The Death of the Virgin Mary; 6) The Last Judgment; 7) Portraits of the donors, the family that originally commissioned the work.

A STORY
FOR ALL TIME

The lesson of Christ's life, like the parables, is timeless. One measure of this quality is the way in which artists of each succeeding age have retold the story in terms of their own time. Hans Memling, in *The Seven* *Joys of Mary (above)*, dating from about 1465 and now in the Pinakothek at Munich, suffused the narrative with the tranquillity of the late medieval Rhineland, yet caught the vibrancy of color surging north from

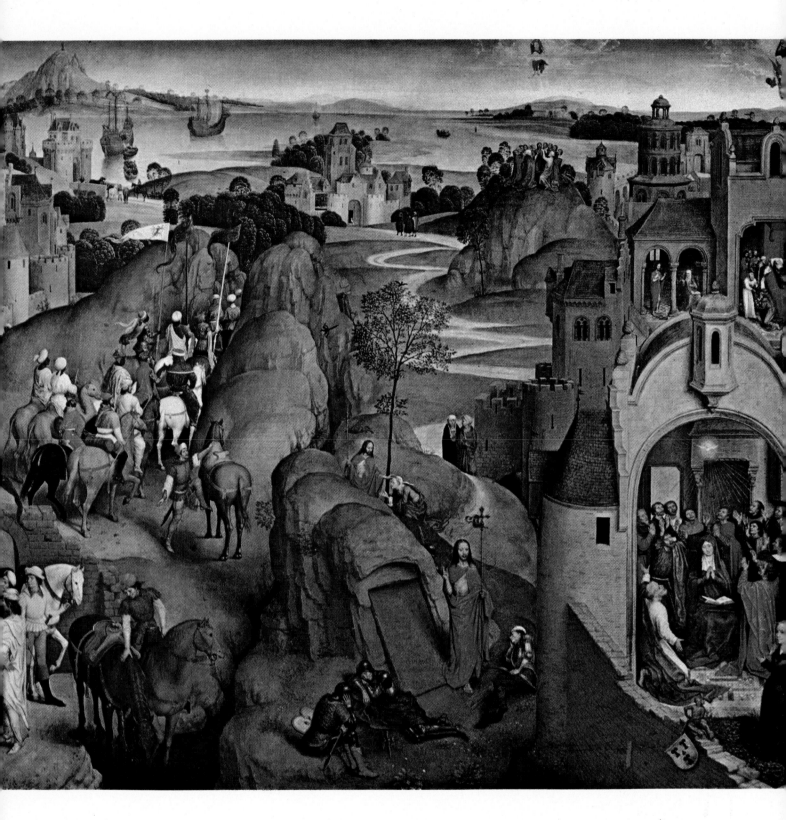

Renaissance Italy. Time runs like a placid river through the painting, uniting the whole, so that each viewing reveals fresh details and new scenes. A few are *(left)* the Annunciation, the angel with the shepherds, the Nativity, and *(right)* the Resurrection and the Ascension of Christ. The Adoration of the Magi fills the center foreground, but the Wise Men are also shown approaching *(at left background)*, confronting Herod in his courtyard *(middle background)*, departing from the manger through a rocky defile and finally setting sail (as John of Hildesheim has embroidered their story) in three ships on their journey home *(background)*.

JOSEPHUS' TESTIMONY

Early nonscriptural works helped to spread the story of Jesus. One of the earliest and most influential of these was written by Flavius Josephus, a Jewish soldier-historian who was born in Jerusalem shortly after Christ died on Calvary. This excerpt from "Antiquities of the Jews" may have been added by another writer.

Now about this time lived Jesus, a wise man, if indeed he should be called a man. He was a doer of wonderful works, a teacher of men who receive the truth with pleasure, and won over many Jews and many Greeks. He was the Christ. And when Pilate, at the information of the leading men among us, sentenced him to the cross, those who loved him at the start did not cease to do so, for he appeared to them alive again on the third day as had been foretold—both this and ten thousand other wonderful things concerning him—by the divine prophets. Nor is the tribe of Christians, so named after him, extinct to this day.

The Letter of Lentulus

What did Jesus look like? No record exists, but writers and artists have tried hard to portray Him. Although now proved to be a 14th or 15th Century work, the description below from the so-called "Letter of Lentulus" is a plausible and enduring word picture of Christ.

Lentulus, president of the people of Jerusalem, to the Roman Senate and People: Greeting.

There has appeared in our times, and still is, a man of great virtue named Christ Jesus, who is called by the Gentiles a prophet of truth, whom his disciples call the Son of God, raising the dead and healing diseases. He is a man of lofty stature, handsome, having a venerable countenance which the beholders can both love and fear. He has wavy hair, rather crisp, of a bluish tinge, and glossy, flowing down from his shoulders, with a parting in the middle of the head after the manner of the Nazarenes. His forehead is even and very serene, and his face without any wrinkle or spot, and beautiful with a slight blush. His nose and mouth are without fault; he has a beard abundant and reddish, of the colour of his hair, not long but forked. His eyes are sparkling and bright. He is terrible in rebuke, calm and loving in admonition, cheerful but preserving gravity, has never been seen to laugh but often to weep. Thus, in stature of body, he is tall; and his hands and limbs are beautiful to look upon. In speech he is grave, reserved, and modest; and he is fair among the children of men. Farewell.

THE KINGDOM WITHIN

Of the countless writings about Christ in the past 2,000 years, few have summed up His legacy as tellingly as the passage below. It was written by the Dutch theologian Johannes Jacobus van der Leeuw (1893-1934) in "The Dramatic History of the Christian Faith."

He came without privileges of outer power or possession to further the work that He was to undertake. He had renounced all those weapons which the man of the world thinks indispensable in his struggle to achieve. He did not stoop to defend Himself when attacked; never in those short but marvellous years of His ministry did He use His superhuman powers to assert Himself. His strength throughout lay in the Kingdom within, not the kingdom without. . . .

His teaching was all woven around the Kingdom of God within, the Kingdom open to all who care to enter—and who prove their ability to fulfil the conditions of entrance. Here no privileges of money or position can bribe the guardians of the sacred Portal, here the Soul of man, alone, naked in the renunciation of all that belongs to the world without, must seek entrance in the strength not of what he has, but of what he is. Rags cannot hide, nor kingly robes impersonate that nobility of the Soul itself, which alone will admit it to the Company of the Elect, the Communion of Saints, who by virtue of their spiritual aristocracy are inhabitants of the Kingdom of God. . . .

Christ, in the crystalline perfection of a life that knew no compromise, showed the way to the Kingdom and the fruits of attainment. It is as if He set out to make clear from the beginning what is essential and what non-essential. Privileges of birth, station, wealth or power He relinquished; efforts to dominate or to convince those around Him He never made; He allowed Himself to be taken, insulted, humiliated, killed to show that all this could not

bar the way to Victory. Never again could any, failing to achieve, blame misfortune or surroundings. Christ in His life took these weak excuses from us, by undergoing all we can undergo and worse, by renouncing from the outset all the weapons we might think indispensable in our quest, and conquering in the strength of the Spirit alone. . . .

That, the teaching He lived, was the essential, the new thing He gave to this world; from that spread Christianity; by that living Fire it is maintained.

Then as now the Christian Faith is centred in the living Christ, then as now His life of love and purity is the way to the Kingdom of God—the way He went, the way we follow.

Joy to the World

The 18th Century English poet Isaac Watts wrote the words (imitating the Psalms) and the 19th Century American composer Lowell Mason wrote the music (in the style of G. F. Handel) of this beloved Christmas hymn.

Joy to the World! The Lord is come; Let earth re - ceive her King; Let

ev - ry— heart— pre - pare— Him— room——, And heav'n and nature—

sing, And— heav'n and na - ture— sing, And— heav'n, and heav'n,— and na - ture sing.

VIII

THE WORLD REBORN

AND I SAW A NEW HEAVEN AND a new earth: for the first heaven and the first earth were passed away; and there was no more sea. And I John saw the holy city, new Jerusalem, coming down from God out of heaven, prepared as a bride adorned for her husband. And I heard a great voice out of heaven saying, Behold, the tabernacle of God is with men, and he will dwell with them, and they shall be his people, and God himself shall be with them, and be their God. And God shall wipe away all tears from their eyes; and there shall be no more death, neither sorrow, nor crying, neither shall there be any more pain: for the former things are passed away. And he that sat upon the throne said, Behold, I make all things new. And he said unto me, Write: for these words are true and faithful. And he said unto me, It is done. I am Alpha and Omega, the beginning and the end.... REVELATION, 21:1-6

A
FRESH
AND RENEWING
FORCE

"HOW SILENTLY, how silently the wondrous gift is given." These familiar words, from the carol "O Little Town of Bethlehem," reflect some of the awe that the birth of Jesus inspires. The words suggest, also, a theological point of view. For, while Christmas is a season of great joy, theologians are quick to point out that it does not exhaust the glory of Christianity. To theologians the Nativity is a beginning whose magnitude must be judged by something that is yet to come.

What happened when Jesus was born, in the eyes of Christians, is that God became incarnate—that He assumed human flesh. "The Word was made flesh," the Gospel according to St. John says, "and dwelt among us." The full significance of the Incarnation, however, was not immediately apparent.

It was not until after the Resurrection, Christians believe, that the meaning of Christmas was unfolded.

A Catholic theologian, Monsignor Myles Bourke, explains it in this way: "We see the full significance of the Incarnation through the Resurrection. When Christ appeared His divinity was concealed behind His human nature. In the Resurrection, there is a transformation of the whole human nature of Jesus." Much the same is stated by a Protestant scholar, Professor W. D. Davies: "The birth of Jesus is the beginning of that mode of His existence which is limited spatially and chronologically. The Resurrection is the beginning of that mode of His existence in which He transcends the limitations of space and time."

The Resurrection, Christians believe, lent a new dimension to the Incarnation; God manifested Himself in human form, and by His suffering and death took man's sins upon Himself and through His Resurrection offered eternal life to those who would but believe in Him.

Incarnation and Resurrection are inextricable. As Professor Davies says: "The stories of the Nativity and the Resurrection embody the idea of the re-creation of the world."

For those who accept this idea, the world is seen afresh. The abbreviated testimony of one believer, the poet Marguerite Wilkinson, accompanies some pictures (on these and the following pages) which show the new, heightened insight into the world about us. Some of the photographs are flooded with sunlight, others clouded in mist. Some evoke a feeling of joy, others a mood of sorrow. Pictorially, they

reflect the message of Christianity.

For Christians preach a religion of joy, but behind the joy lies an awareness of sorrow. The life of Jesus drawn from the Scriptures is a story of love and salvation achieved through pain and humiliation. Thus, while the triumphant "Hallelujah Chorus" is the best-known part of Handel's oratorio *Messiah,* it is still only a part. Handel turned to the Old Testament prophet Isaiah to find words to describe what God in human flesh faced on earth. The prophet says (53:3,5), in this passage which many Christians relate to Jesus: "He is despised and rejected of men; a man of sorrows, and acquainted with grief . . . he was wounded for our transgressions, he was bruised for our iniquities."

But for Christians the sorrow is dispelled and the joy of Christmas triumphs in the final accounting. Jesus said (John 16:20): ". . . ye shall weep and lament, but the world shall rejoice: and ye shall be sorrowful, but your sorrow shall be turned into joy." For Christians believe that something new entered the world when the Child was born. And they believe that something new—a gospel of love and eternal life—is the heritage of all who will accept the love of God through Jesus. And they believe, as St. Paul wrote (Romans 8:38-39): "Neither death, nor life, nor angels, nor principalities, nor powers, nor things present, nor things to come, nor height, nor depth, nor any other creature, shall be able to separate us from the love of God, which is in Christ Jesus our Lord."

Out of the troubled dark I came...

Time narrowed then
Into an instant....
And quietly my spirit was renewed...

Time widened out into eternity;
Power was upon me so that I could see
Light beyond light...
Torrents of tumbled glory....

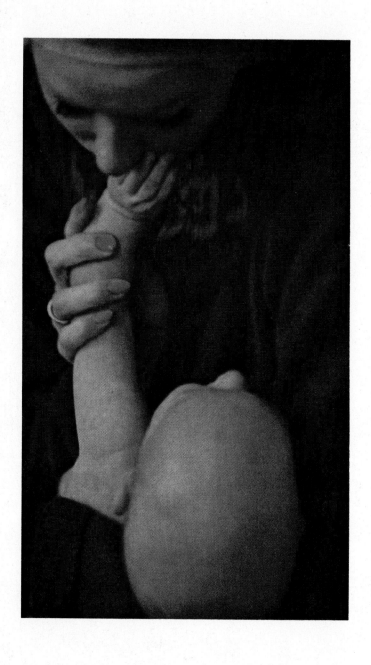

White rays impetuous, violet pools serene...
And a broad azure tide whose waves are curled
Around the margins of the farthest world.
Light followed darkness...

IN THIS VOLUME
ANTHOLOGY SELECTIONS

CHRISTMAS MUSIC

INDEX

* *This symbol preceding a page number indicates a photograph or painting of the subject mentioned*

PICTURE CREDITS

Illustrations on each page are listed from left to right and from top to bottom. In the case of paintings and works of sculpture, the artist's name, if known, is given in capitals—e.g., FRA ANGELICO; the name of the photographer or the picture agency appears in parentheses—e.g., (William J. Sumits).

Frontispiece: The Four Evangelists, Gospel Book of Charlemagne, French, illuminated Eighth Century by GODESSALC, Rhenane School, Bibliothèque Nationale, Paris. 8—Isaiah from the high altar, 18th Century Benedictine Church at Zwiefalten, Germany (Walter Sanders). 10—Tree of Jesse, Psalter, English, 13th Century. M. 43, Pierpont Morgan Library, New York. 11—Tree of Jesse, Psalter of Ingeborg, French, 13th Century. Musée Condé, Chantilly (William J. Sumits). 12, 13—Efrem Ilani, map by Fritz Kredel. 14, 15—Manouq, David Rubinger. 16, 17—Fritz Schlesinger. 18, 19—Dmitri Kessel. 20—Drawing by Nicholas Solovioff. 21—Woodcuts by Fritz Kredel. 22—Detail, Annunciation to the Virgin, St. Columba Altarpiece, 15th Century. ROGIER VAN DER WEYDEN, Alte Pinakothek, Munich (Joachim Blauel). 24—The Annunciation, 15th Century. Veronese miniature, Budapest Museum of Fine Arts (Harry N. Abrams, Inc., New York). 25—Annunciation to the Virgin, 15th Century. FRA ANGELICO, Diocesan Museum, Cortona, Italy (Eric Schaal). 26, 27—Merode Altarpiece, 15th Century. MASTER OF FLEMALLE, Metropolitan Museum of Art, The Cloisters Collection, Purchase. 28, 29—Details from Merode Altarpiece (Dmitri Kessel). 30—Drawings by Nicholas Solovioff. 31—Woodcuts by Fritz Kredel. 32—Nativity, 13th Century. French, Chartres Cathedral, France (Dmitri Kessel). 34—Christ Child Adoration, Miniature from Book of Hours, French, 15th Century. MS. 288, Walters Art Gallery, Baltimore. 35—Adoration of the Infant, 15th Century illumination from *The Golden Legend* by Jacobus de Voragine, Bibliothèque Nationale, Paris. 36—Vierge Dorée, 13th Century. Amiens Cathedral, France (Howard Sochurek). 37—Madonna and Child, Seventh Century, Church of Santa Maria Novella (Santa Francesca Romana), Rome. 38—Garden of Paradise, MASTER OF THE UPPER RHINE, early 15th Century. Städelsches Kunstinstitut, Frankfurt, Germany (Joachim Blauel). 39—Madonna Enthroned, early 15th Century. JAN VAN EYCK, Gemäldegalerie, Staatliche Kunstsammlungen, Dresden, Germany (Larry Burrows). 40—Bulto from Watrous, New Mexico, 19th Century. Taylor Museum of the Colorado Springs Fine Arts Center (L. H. Benschneider), Round woodcarving, 20th Century. DAVID CHITUKU (Society for the Propagation of the Bible, London). 41—The Nativity, JON LU HUNG NIEN, Catholic University, Peking (Dr. W. B. Pettus). 42, 43—18th Century Neapolitan Crèche (David Lees for TIME). 47—Woodcuts by Fritz Kredel. 48—Choir of Angels, late 15th Century. BENOZZO GOZZOLI, Medici-Ricardi Palace, courtesy Superintendent of Florence Art Galleries (Fernand Bourges). 50, 51—Rejoicing Angel, Marginal medallion from French Book of Hours, early 15th Century. MS. 288, Walters Art Gallery, Choir of Five Angels, Detail from the Nativity, late 15th Century. PIERO DELLA FRANCESCA, National Gallery, London (Dmitri Kessel). 52, 53—Three Angels with Instruments, Frame of center panel, Linaioli Altarpiece, early 15th Century. FRA ANGELICO, Museum of San Marco, Florence (Scala, Florence). 54, 55—Freudenaltar, late 15th Century. MASTER ARNT, Church of St. Nicholas, Calcar, Germany (Landesbildstelle, Düsseldorf). 56, 57—Drawings by Nicholas Solovioff. 59—Woodcuts by Fritz Kredel. 60—

Annunciation to the Shepherds, early 15th Century. MEISTER DER GOLDENEN TAFEL, Landesmuseum, Hanover (Hans Nölter). 62—Annunciation to the Shepherds, 15th Century. Miniature from St. George's Script No. 28, Badische Landesbibliothek, Karlsruhe, Germany. 63—Annunciation to the Shepherds, 15th Century. SANO DI PIETRO, Siena Pinacoteca, Siena, Italy (Scala, Florence). 64—Kalendrier des Bergiers, Paris 15th Century. Bibliothèque Nationale, Paris (New York Public Library). 65—Annunciation to the Shepherds, Grandes Heures de la Famille de Rohan, MS. Lat. 9471, Bibliothèque Nationale, Paris. 66, 67—Adoration of the Shepherds, Dutch woodcarving, end of 15th Century. Rijksmuseum, Amsterdam (Foto-Commissie), Adoration of the Shepherds, late 15th Century. CARLO CRIVELLI, Strasbourg Museum, France (Larry Burrows for TIME). 69—Woodcuts by Fritz Kredel. 70—procession of the Magi, late 15th Century. BENOZZO GOZZOLI, Medici-Ricardi Palace, courtesy Superintendent of Florence Art Galleries (Fernand Bourges). 72—Meeting of the Three Kings, early 15th Century. Miniature from the Très Riches Heures du Duc de Berry, Musée Condé, Chantilly (Giraudon). 73—Journey of the Three Kings, Detail of Tympanum, Southwest portal, Ulm Cathedral, Evangelisches Dekanatsamt (Dmitri Kessel). 74—Adoration of the Magi, late 13th Century. PIETRO CAVALLINI, Santa Maria in Trastevere, Rome (Scala, Florence). 75—Detail of Gifts from Adoration of the Magi, unknown painter, Dutch School, c. 1500. Kaiser Wilhelm Museum, Krefeld, Germany (Hein Engelskirchen)—drawing by Eva Cellini. 76, 77—Adoration of the Magi, late 15th Century. SANDRO BOTTICELLI, National Gallery of Art, Washington, D.C., Mellon Collection (Beck Engraving Co.). 78, 79—Sleep of the Three Kings, 12th Century. GISELBERTUS, Cathedral of St.-Lazare, Autun, France, courtesy *Giselbertus, Sculptor of Autun*—Orion Press and *The Story of the Wise Men*—Young Scott (Franceschi Trianon Press). 80 through 84—Illustrations from "Leben der Heiligen drei Königen" in the Pierpont Morgan Library, from *The Story of the Three Kings*—*Melchior-Balthasar-Jaspar* by John of Hildesheim retold by Margaret B. Freeman. The Metropolitan Museum of Art, New York. 85—Woodcuts by Fritz Kredel. 86—Christ's Ascension, early 14th Century. GIOTTO, Arena Chapel, Padua, Italy, courtesy Superintendent of Monuments, Venice (Fernand Bourges and Robert Kafka). 88—Christ's Entry into Jerusalem, miniature from The Urbino Bible, St. Louis University. 89—Head of Christ, 1931. GEORGES ROUAULT, Cleveland Museum of Art. 90, 91—Interior Wings, Isenheim Altar, Matthias Grünewald, Unterlinden Museen of Colmar, France (Eric Schaal). 92, 93—Life of Christ, COLOGNE MASTER, Staatliches Museen, Berlin-Dahlem (Raymond and Raymond, Inc.). 94, 95—The Seven Joys of Mary, 15th Century. HANS MEMLING, Alte Pinakothek, Munich (Joachim Blauel). 96—Drawing by Nicholas Soloviof. 97—Woodcuts by Fritz Kredel. 98—Garry Winogrand. 100—Kenneth Hine. 101, 102—John De Visser. 103—Dennis Hallinan from Free Lance Photographers Guild. 104, 105—Emil Schulthess from Black Star. 106, 107—Dan Budnik from Magnum, Kosti Ruohamaa from Black Star.

FOR FURTHER READING

Bibles: *The New Testament Octapla,* "Eight English Versions of the New Testament in the Tyndale-King James Tradition," edited by Luther A. Weigle, Thomas Nelson and Sons, 1962; Revised Standard Version, Thomas Nelson and Sons; Douay version, Douay Bible House, 1941; The New Testament, translated by R. A. Knox, Sheed & Ward, 1954; The New Testament, edited by the Episcopal Committee of the Confraternity of Christian Doctrine, St. Anthony Guild Press, 1953.

Bornkamm, Günther, *Jesus of Nazareth.* Harper & Bros., 1961.

Burrows, Millar, *More Light on the Dead Sea Scrolls.* Viking Press, 1958.

Comay, Joan, *Everyone's Guide to Israel.* Doubleday & Co., 1962.

Croft, Aloysius, ed., *The Mystery of Christmas.* Bruce Publishing Co., 1956.

Daniel-Rops, Henri, *The Book of Mary.* Hawthorn Books, 1960. *Daily Life in the Time of Jesus.* Hawthorn Books, 1962.

De Robeck, Nesta, *The Christmas Crib.* Bruce Publishing Co., 1959.

De Vaux, Roland, *Ancient Israel.* McGraw-Hill Book Co., 1961.

Ferguson, George, *Signs and Symbols in Christian Art.* Oxford University Press, 1954.

Freeman, Margaret B., *The Story of the Three Kings* (originally written by John of Hildesheim in the 14th Century). Metropolitan Museum of Art, 1955.

FOR FURTHER READING *continued*

Fuller, Reginald H., *The New Testament in Current Study.* Charles Scribner's Sons, 1962.

Grabar, Andre, and Carl Nordenfalk, *Early Medieval Painting.* Skira, 1957.

Grant, Robert M., *The Earliest Lives of Jesus.* Harper & Bros., 1961.

Hastings, James, *Dictionary of the Bible* (rev. ed. by Frederick C. Grant and H. H. Rowley). Charles Scribner's Sons, 1963.

James, M. R., *The Apocryphal New Testament.* Oxford University Press, 1955.

Jobé, Joseph, *Ecce Homo.* Harper & Row, 1962.

Mâle, Emile, *Religious Art from the Twelfth to the Eighteenth Century.* Pantheon, 1949.

May, Herbert G., ed., *Oxford Bible Atlas.* Oxford University Press, 1962.

Morey, Charles Rufus, *Early Christian Art.* Princeton University Press, 1953.

Muilenberg, James, *The Way of Israel.* Harper & Row, 1961.

Puech, H. C. and other translators, *The Gospel According to Thomas.* Harper & Bros., 1959.

Rice, D. Talbot, *The Beginnings of Christian Art.* Abingdon Press, 1957.

Sheed, F. J., ed., *The Mary Book.* Sheed & Ward, 1950.

Shrady, M. L., ed., *In the Spirit of Wonder.* Pantheon Books, 1961.

Tillich, Paul, *The New Being.* Charles Scribner's Sons, 1955.

Timmermans, Felix, *The Christ Child in Flanders.* Henry Regnery, 1960.

ACKNOWLEDGMENTS

The editors of this volume are particularly indebted to Monsignor Myles M. Bourke, Professor of New Testament, St. Joseph's Seminary, Dunwoodie, Yonkers, New York, and Professor W. D. Davies, Edward Robinson Professor of Biblical Theology, Union Theological Seminary, New York, New York, who read and commented on the complete text; to Byron Dobell, who initiated the project and saw it through its earliest stages; and to Daniel Longwell, former Chairman of the Board of Editors of LIFE. In the early planning the editors were also assisted by the perceptive comments of Dr. Tom F. Driver, Union Theological Seminary, Monsignor Timothy J. Flynn, Archdiocese of New York, Professor Henri M. Peyre, Yale University, and Dr. J. Carter Swaim, Department of the English Bible, National Council of the Churches of Christ in the U.S.A. The editors are also grateful to the Reverend Lowrie John Daly, S.J., Saint Louis University; The Metropolitan Museum of Art and the Pierpont Morgan Library, New York; the Walters Art Gallery, Baltimore; to the numerous European museums, libraries and art galleries cited in the credits on page 111, and to the many individuals who generously contributed valuable assistance.

Grateful acknowledgment is made for permission to reprint, in whole or in part, selections from the following:

P. 20 *The Prophets,* Abraham J. Heschel. Harper & Row, Publishers, Inc., New York, 1962.

P. 30 "On the Annunciation of Fra Angelico," Manuel Machado. Translated from the Spanish by Thomas Walsh. Reprinted by permission of Mrs. Edward M. Walsh.
The Christ Child in Flanders, Felix Timmermans. Copyright 1960. The Henry Regnery Company, Chicago.

P. 31 "Annunciation to Mary," Rainer Maria Rilke. From *Translations from the Poetry of Rainer Maria Rilke,* M. D. Herter Norton. Copyright © 1938 by W. W. Norton & Company, Inc. By permission of W. W. Norton & Company, Inc., New York, and Hogarth Press, London.
English translation of lyrics for "The Angel Gabriel" from the *University Carol Book,* edited by Eric Routley, copyright 1961 by H. Freeman and Co., Brighton, England; permission granted by Mills Music Inc. for U.S.A. and Canada.

P. 44 "The Gospel of James." From *The Apocryphal Gospels,* B. Harris Cowper. Williams and Norgate, London, 1870. By permission of Ernest Benn, Ltd., London.
"A Gothic Noel," Jehan Le Povremoyne. Translated and adapted from the French by permission of the author.

P. 56 "An Iconography of Heavenly Beings," Gilbert Highet. From *Horizon* Magazine, copyright 1960 by American Heritage Publishing Company, Inc.

P. 57 "Christmas Eve," Robert Bridges. Reprinted by permission of The Clarendon Press, Oxford.

P. 58 Introduction to *The Shepherd Who Missed the Manger,* Rufus M. Jones. By permission of the Girard Trust Corn Exchange Bank, Philadelphia, Executors of the Estate of Rufus M. Jones.
Dream Days, Kenneth Grahame. By permission of the Kenneth Grahame Estate and the Bodley Head, London.

P. 68 "The Gospel of Pseudo-Matthew." From *The Apocryphal Gospels,* B. Harris Cowper. Williams and Norgate, London, 1870. By permission of Ernest Benn, Ltd., London.

"The Friendly Beasts," 12th Century English carol. Adaptation copyright, 1958, by G. Schirmer, Inc. Reprinted by permission.

"Le Grant Kalendrier des Bergiers." From *A Christmas Book: An Anthology for Moderns,* compiled by D. B. Wyndham Lewis and G. C. Heseltine. Published by E. P. Dutton & Company, Inc., New York and reprinted with their permission. Reprinted also with permission of J. M. Dent & Sons, Ltd., London.

P. 69 English translation of lyrics for "The Carol of the Bagpipers" from the *University Carol Book,* edited by Eric Routley, copyright 1961 by H. Freeman and Co., Brighton, England; permission granted by Mills Music Inc. for U.S.A. and Canada.

P. 80 *The Story of the Three Kings,* Margaret B. Freeman. Copyright 1955, The Metropolitan Museum of Art, New York.

P. 82 "Journey of the Magi," from *Collected Poems 1909-1935* by T. S. Eliot, copyright 1936, by Harcourt, Brace & World, Inc. Reprinted by permission of the publishers, and by permission of Faber and Faber, Ltd., Publishers, London.

P. 83 "Nicolas Roi Mage." From *Vent de Terre,* Roger Vercel. Translated and adapted with permission from the publisher, Editions Albin Michel, Paris.

P. 84 "Frankincense and Myrrh," copyright by Heywood Hale Broun. Reprinted by permission of Heywood Hale Broun and Constance Broun.

P. 85 "The Golden Carol" from the collection *Noels* by Marx and Anne Oberndorfer, copyright 1932, H. T. FitzSimons Company, Chicago.

P. 96 *Jerusalem and Rome: The Writings of Josephus,* selected and introduced by Nahum N. Glatzer, copyright 1960 by The World Publishing Company. By permission of Meridian Books, The World Publishing Company, Cleveland and New York.
"The Letter of Lentulus." From *The Apocryphal Gospels,* B. Harris Cowper. Williams and Norgate, London, 1870. By permission of Ernest Benn, Ltd., London.
The Dramatic History of the Christian Faith, J. J. van der Leeuw. The Theosophical Publishing House, Madras, 1927.

Production Staff for Time Incorporated

Arthur R. Murphy Jr. (Vice President and Director of Production)

Robert E. Foy, James P. Menton and Caroline Ferri

Body text photocomposed under the direction of

Albert J. Dunn and Arthur J. Dunn

X